Uruguay against Brazil in the 1950 World Cup Final

ULTIMATE FOOTBALL

Ivor Baddiel

DORLING KINDERSLEY
London • New York • Moscow • Sydney

A DORLING KINDERSLEY BOOK

Project Editor Jane Donnelly

Editor Rachel Wardley

Art Editors Sharon Grant and Ivan Finnegan

Deputy Managing Editor Dawn Sirett

Managing Art Editor
C. David Gillingwater

DTP Designers Nicola Studdart and
Cordelia Springer

Production Ruth Cobb

Picture Research Sam Ruston

Consultant Keir Radnedge

Published in Great Britain by
Dorling Kindersley Limited,
9 Henrietta Street, London WC2E 8PS

4 6 8 10 9 7 5 3

Visit us on the World Wide Web at http://www.dk.com
Copyright © 1998 Dorling Kindersley Limited, London

Main Laws of the Game pp 90-91 taken from the 1997 Laws of the Game
copyright © 1997 FIFA. Adapted with the kind permission of FIFA.

A CIP catalogue record for this book
is available from the British Library.

ISBN: 0-7513-5655-7

Colour reproduction by
GRB, Italy
Printed and bound in Italy
by Graphicom

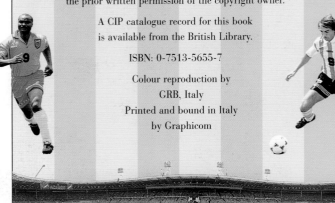

PASSION

ACTION

SKILLS

THE BEST GAME IN THE WORLD

Football is the world's favourite game, and it's not hard to understand why. Football is easy to follow, it's fast and exciting, you only really need a ball to play it, it can be played by any number of boys and girls, anywhere and anytime, and it brings people together from all over the world. And those are only some of its attractions!

The FIFA World Cup is the ultimate highlight for every football fan and every player, so it's not surprising that the World Cup features on several pages of *Ultimate Football*. But football is about more than just the World Cup, and in the following pages you will be able to read about the great teams and great players, the stadiums, the cups, and the competitions that have given our game such a colourful past and which promise so much for the future.

In all this excitement, it's important not to forget one thing in football: the game loses much of its enjoyment if we don't remember the rules of Fair Play. Playing fair makes football much more fun, and it makes winning all the more satisfying. When you turn these pages and see the stars of the past and present, you can't help realising that the great players didn't need to foul or cheat to prove how good they were.

No matter how much of a football freak you may be, I'm sure you will find a lot in *Ultimate Football* that you didn't know about the game. There's always plenty to learn! That's another reason why we all think football is simply the best game in the world, and always will be.

SEPP BLATTER
General Secretary of FIFA

TO ALL FOOTBALL FANS

Football is the greatest game in the world, of that I am in no doubt. At whatever level, there is no greater feeling than being out on the pitch running around, scoring a goal, making a fantastic save, playing a perfect pass, or executing a brilliantly timed tackle. But, however much we love to play, sadly the whistle blows or the park shuts and it's all over. But that's no reason to stop thinking about football or to stop building up your football knowledge. This book has enough information in it to satisfy every football fan. From how to become a professional to who scored the winning goal in the 1938 World Cup Final, it's all in here. So when the referee's whistle blows again or the park gates open, as you score that goal, make that save, play that pass, or execute that tackle, you'll not only be able to imagine that you are Pele, Banks, Platini, or Beckenbauer, you'll also know the game it happened in, the stadium it was played in, the number of people who were in the crowd, what the date was, what the final score was, and anything else that's needed to make sure that your footballing imagination is as good as your footballing feet or hands.

GIANLUCA VIALLI
Chelsea Manager and Italian international

CONTENTS

Jules Rimet trophy

THE GAME

Football player from the 1800s

Dribbling the ball

Maracana Stadium, Rio de Janeiro

GREAT TEAMS

Match programmes

Brazil after winning the 1958 World Cup

Germany's team badge

Michel Platini

GREAT PLAYERS

Ronaldo playing for Barcelona

Pele in 1970

THE FIFA WORLD CUP

1966 World Cup action

1994 FIFA World Cup mascot

Dino Zoff

1994 Brazil team

An illustration of football in the 1500s

THE GAME

Football is a massive industry. For the lucky few who participate the
rewards are great, but football is about more than just the players and
the managers. It's about the fans, the stadiums, the trophies, the referees,
and many other aspects that make it a game loved by millions.

HISTORY

An illustration of a street football match in England in 1721

FOOTBALL AS WE KNOW IT TODAY developed in England. However, no one can be certain when a round object was first kicked towards another person, as games involving a ball, teams, and some form of scoring have been around for centuries. About 3000 years ago, the ancient Chinese played a game known as Tsu Chu (Tsu means kicking and Chu means a stuffed ball of animal skin). At about the same time in Japan they played Kemari, which involved players trying to kick a ball through two bamboo shoots. The ancient Greeks had a game called Episkyros and the Romans brought the game of Harpascum to Britain, which may have developed into football. By AD 217 in Britain, games involving whole villages certainly existed. These games had no rules and were often so violent that a number of kings tried to have them banned. Fortunately for the future of football, the games were too popular and people played on despite the bans.

An illustration from the late 1800s of an English football player

STREET VIOLENCE
The earliest record of a football match in Britain dates back to the 1100s. Throughout the Middle Ages, the chances of actually seeing the ball in what was then called football were very slim. In fact, simply watching a game would have been difficult, as it bore more resemblance to a full scale riot than to the relatively calm spectacle of today. People were often seriously hurt and, with no stretchers to ferry them to the sidelines, they were likely to be trampled underfoot as the game continued.

This Japanese print from 1897 shows a group of Samurai warriors watching a ceremonial game of Kemari. Kemari developed from ancient Chinese football.

RULES, WHO NEEDS RULES?

By the early 1800s in Britain, any number of different versions of football were being played in private schools. With no agreement on team, pitch, or goal sizes, and in some cases, handling allowed, it was impossible for schools to play each other or for the game to be played after leaving school. Thus it was that in 1848 fourteen students from Cambridge University came together to thrash out some rules. Though not universally accepted, these rules were the first attempt to give some uniformity to the game. Other rules were subsequently drawn up. The major stumbling block to achieving an agreed set of rules was whether to allow the use of hands. To decide on this, 11 representatives of clubs in London got together on 26 October 1863 to form the Football Association (FA). By 8 December that year they had agreed a set of rules.

British private schools laid the foundations for the development of a common set of football rules. The Harrow School team (shown above in 1867) were among the first to play to the FA rules that were agreed in 1863.

Football supporters have always been noisy and enthusiastic. In the early days, they used rattles.

Charles Alcock, one of the early secretaries of the English FA

Left, illustrations from the late 1800s showing how to chest the ball and how not to head the ball. Note the large size of the ball compared to the modern version.

FOOTBALL'S FIRST CUP COMPETITION

As football continued to grow in Britain, it wasn't long before a knockout cup competition was suggested. In 1871 the then secretary of the English FA, Charles Alcock, proposed a tournament based on one that had been played at Harrow School. The following year the world's oldest football cup competition, the English FA Cup, was born. The competition was completed in just 13 matches. Wanderers upset the form books by beating favourites Royal Engineers 1-0 in the Final, which was watched by 2000 spectators.

From the very beginning, important FA Cup matches attracted huge crowds and they continue to do so today.

THE ENGLISH LEAGUE

In 1885 the English FA legalized professionalism, allowing clubs to pay players. This meant that more games needed to be played to pay players' salaries. William McGregor of Aston Villa proposed the idea of home and away fixtures. It was adopted by 12 clubs and on 22 March 1888 the English Football League was formed.

William McGregor, founder of the English Football League

One of the early English League medals won by Aston Villa in 1897

When English players became professionals their salaries were paid out of match ticket sales. FA Cup matches also helped to support players' salaries. The FA Cup Final in 1901 (above) drew a record crowd of 114,815 to see Tottenham Hotspur play Sheffield United. The match was drawn, but Tottenham won the replay.

As the game grew in popularity, a wide range of books and souvenirs was produced to satisfy the fans' demands.

A GREAT EXPORT

Britain was responsible for the introduction of football to many other parts of the world. The first place to be infected was Argentina when, in 1865, British residents founded the Buenos Aires Football Club. In 1879 the English Football Club was set up in Denmark, and in Switzerland students who had learnt the game from their British counterparts set up St. Gallen Football Club. In 1880 British businessmen set up a club in Germany. The worldwide spread of the game had begun.

FIFA IS FORMED

By 1903 there was talk of creating an international football federation, and in 1904 the Federation Internationale de Football Association, or FIFA, was formed. Football continued to grow worldwide, most notably in Europe and South America, and by 1939 membership of FIFA had grown to more than 50 countries.

Today membership of FIFA stands at almost 200 nations, making football the world's greatest game.

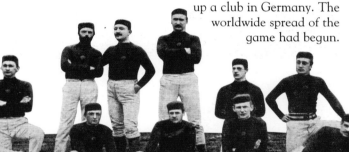

Football was first played in Denmark in the late 1800s. The first Copenhagen team for the 1886-87 season is shown above.

FROM SIMPLE BEGINNINGS

Football has come a long way in the last 150 years. Television coverage and sponsorship have turned it into a multi-billion pound global industry. The top players are now media stars worth millions and they have dedicated physiotherapists and trainers to help them maintain optimum levels of fitness.

Football training consisted of a brisk walk for the 1906 West Bromwich Albion team. The training facilities on offer to players have changed a great deal since then.

THEN AND NOW

IF YOU WERE TO TRAVEL back in time and stumble upon a football match in the 1890s, things would not be that unfamiliar. The essence of the game has remained the same. However, since that time, football has seen changes. It is now the world's most popular sport and has spawned a huge range of merchandise and memorabilia. Over the decades, changing fashions and the availability of new materials have transformed the basic kit, and huge sums of money have been invested in research to produce the most skill-enhancing balls and boots.

MERCHANDISE
At one time, the only place you would see pictures of footballers, other than in newspapers, was on cigarette cards. Today it's possible to buy almost anything, from bedsheets to clocks and bottles of wine, displaying the latest stars.

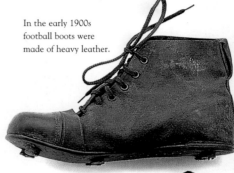

In the early 1900s football boots were made of heavy leather.

PROGRAMMES

Over the years, programmes have become glossy colour magazines, crammed with action pictures, facts, and figures.

The earliest programmes were very basic, consisting of just one sheet of paper. Today they are more like magazines, but the early ones are considerably more valuable.

Match cards, such as this one from 1875, were the forerunners of today's magazine-style programmes.

Today football boots are designed to give comfort and maximum performance.

BOOTS
In the 1800s before football boots were widely available, some players nailed studs into their ordinary working boots. Today's boots are sleek and colourful compared to the early heavy leather ankle-length boots.

TICKET PRICES
A ticket for the first official international match between England and Scotland in 1872 cost one shilling (five pence). The cheapest tickets for an England match during the 1996 European Championship cost £15. The most expensive were £130.

This illustration from the 1600s shows the bladder of a "pallone", an early Italian football, being inflated.

Below, a modern-day football used in the 1996 European Championship.

FOOTBALLS

The first footballs were animal bladders encased in leather. They were laced together by hand and often lost their shape during a game. They were also prone to water retention, making them increase in weight considerably if it rained. Modern footballs use a number of different materials and have a plastic coating, which avoids the problem of water retention. They are lighter and tend to keep their shape well.

The pre-1940s football (above) wasn't waterproof and the final seam had to be laced up.

In the early 1900s shorts and shirts were long.

In the 1950s shirts resembled rugby shirts.

By the 1970s shorts were shorter and shirts slim-fitting.

Short lengths continue to vary from one decade to the next. These are from the 1980s.

Today shorts are mid-length. Shirts are loose-fitting.

SHIRTS

Football shirts have changed a great deal over the years. At one time they were made of cotton, had lace-up collars, and no writing on them. Nowadays they are made of synthetic material, which in some cases has been specifically designed to give maximum ventilation. They will almost inevitably bear a sponsor's name on the front.

SHORTS

The main change to shorts has been their length. At one time they were knee-length, but today's footballer wears them somewhat shorter.

GLOVES

Originally, goalkeepers wore simple, cotton gloves. Today's gloves have heavy padding, textured surfaces, and adhesive strips to keep them on.

Modern goalkeepers' gloves have lots of padding.

FOOTBALL GAMES

Blow football and table football were the first games to try and recreate real football in people's living rooms. Although they are still enjoyed, today's advanced technology means that the computer screen, rather than the floor or table, now dominates football's indoor playing arena.

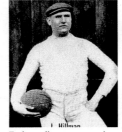

Early goalkeepers wore plain shirts and shorts.

Modern goalkeepers wear colourful strips.

GOALKEEPERS' KIT

Until recently, goalkeepers' shirts were green, yellow, or white. They have undergone great changes and are now multi-coloured and padded.

RULES AND RULE CHANGES

THE BASIC AIM OF FOOTBALL has remained the same but it is a developing game. At one time no substitutes were allowed, a referee could award a goal if a player used his hands to stop a ball from crossing the goal line, and the goalkeeper could pick up the ball from a back pass. Since 1913, agreed international rules have been in operation, but over the years there have been many changes. Some have had a profound effect on the game, whilst others have just tweaked it a little. In general, the intention is to create an exciting spectacle in which those officiating can do their jobs with clarity and consistency.

Referees and assistant referees have the difficult task of balancing rules with creating exciting, flowing football.

SOME CHANGES FOR THE BETTER

1913: Opposing players to go back 10 yards (9.2 metres) when a free kick is being taken.
1924: Away strips to be worn by the visiting team if strip colours are the same.
1925: Players to have two feet on the ground when taking a throw-in.
1937: Arc of circle drawn outside the penalty area.
1951: Obstruction included as an offence punishable by an indirect free kick.
1976: Red and yellow cards introduced.
1981: Three points for a win introduced.
1989: A player level with the last outfield defender is no longer offside.
1992: Pass back rule introduced. The goalkeeper is not allowed to pick the ball up if it is kicked back by one of his or her own players.

A referee cautioning a player with a yellow card.

A corner kick is taken from the corner arc next to the flag.

THE SIMPLEST GAME RULES OF 1862 (ADOPTED BY FIFA IN 1863)
1. A goal is scored whenever the ball is forced through the goal and under the bar, except be it thrown by hand.
2. Hands may be used only to stop the ball and place it on the ground before the feet.
3. Kicks must be aimed only at the ball.
4. A player may not kick at the ball whilst it is in the air.
5. No tripping up or heel kicking is allowed.
6. Whenever the ball is kicked beyond the side flags, it must be returned by the player who kicked it, from the spot where it passed the flag line, in a straight line towards the middle of the ground.
7. When a ball is kicked behind the line of the goal, it shall be kicked off from that line by one of the side whose goal it is.
8. No opposite player may stand within six paces of the kicker when he is kicking off.
9. A player is out of play (offside) immediately he is in front of the ball, and he must return behind the ball as soon as possible. If the ball be kicked by his own side past a player, he may not touch it, kick it nor advance until one of the other side has first kicked it or one of his own side having followed it up, has been able, when in front of him, to kick it.
10. No charging is allowed when a player is out of play, i.e., immediately the ball is behind him.

Since 1913, opposing players have been made to stand 10 yards (9.2 metres) from where a free kick is taken.

THE FUTURE

The game continues to evolve. It is unlikely that the use of hands is ever going to be permitted, but who knows what lies ahead? Here are some possible changes.

Video Referees: Video could have a major part to play in the future of football refereeing.
Sin Bin: A third card may be introduced allowing the referee to order a player to leave the pitch for ten minutes.
Offside: A heated issue; some advocate abolishing the offside rule altogether.

Another future change could see the current throw-in replaced with a kick-in.

TECHNIQUES AND TACTICS

Whatever position you play in, there are many techniques that need to be mastered. Positional play if you're a goalkeeper, the timing of a tackle if you're a defender, accurate passing if you're a midfielder, and beating your marker if you're an attacker are just some of the many different skills players need to work on. Here are some of the key techniques to learn.

Goalkeeping

The best goalkeepers are extremely agile and have razor-sharp reflexes. As a goalkeeper your main priority is to stop the ball going into the net. When making a save, any part of your body can be utilized, but your main assets will always be your hands.

When catching a high ball, form your hands into a "w" shape with your fingers spread out and your thumbs nearly touching. Your forearms should be slightly bent to take the power out of the shot.

STOPPING THE BALL

A goalkeeper should always try leaping up to catch high shots. If you cannot catch a high ball, it is best to punch it out, using both fists clenched tightly together. For chest-high shots, place yourself in line with the ball and cushion the shot with your body, cupping your hands around the ball. For shots out of your immediate reach, you may have to dive and palm the ball away, angling your hands to divert the ball round the post or over the bar.

Goalkeepers need to anticipate where the ball is going and move quickly into position to stop the shot.

Zoff, playing for Italy, shouts instructions to the rest of his defence.

Schmeichel closes the angle to try to block Vialli's goal in a match between Manchester United and Chelsea.

COMMANDING THE GOAL AREA

A goalkeeper must command his or her defence confidently. It is vital that defenders know when to leave the ball for the keeper, when to pass it back, or when to kick it out of play. Any shout must be clear and loud.

POSITIONAL PLAY

As a goalkeeper it is crucial to concentrate at all times, positioning yourself so that you are always between the ball and the goal. If an attacker is heading straight towards the goal, it is important to "narrow the angle". This means gradually moving towards the ball, giving the attacker less of the goal to aim at.

Defending

As a defender it is your job to stop opposing attackers gaining possession of the ball and to start to build an attack for your own team. It is a role that demands coordination, as well as strength and determination.

Always watch the ball when tackling.

Aldair of Portuguese club Benfica closely marking Ruud Gullit of AC Milan in the European Cup Final in 1990

MARKING

Marking involves staying close to an opponent to stop them from passing, shooting, or receiving the ball. When marking another player, it is important to remain between that player and the goal, or "goalside" as it is known. The attacker will try and get away from you, so you must concentrate not just on where the ball is, but also on where the attacker is going.

A good marker will deny an opponent the space he needs to use the ball well.

BLOCK TACKLE

There are two main tackles, a block tackle and a sliding tackle. To block tackle, strike the ball just as your opponent is about to pass it. Using all your weight, put the inside of your foot as near to the centre of the ball as possible. You need to remain on your feet so you can gain possession of the ball after winning the tackle.

Croatia's Vlaovic, the victim of a sliding tackle by Portugal's Sousa

SLIDING TACKLE

A successful sliding tackle requires expert timing. It is used to clear the ball rather than gain possession. When your opponent has the ball, run towards them and slide into the tackle. Bend your supporting leg whilst stretching out the other one.

When heading the ball, move in to meet the ball. Don't wait for the ball to come to you.

DEFENSIVE HEADING

A defensive header is meant to clear the ball as far away as possible. The timing of your run and jump is very important in order to get as much power into the header as possible and the more height you can get into your jump, the better. Remember to use your forehead, to head the ball upwards, and to always hit the bottom half of the ball.

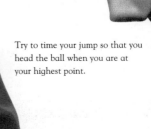

Try to time your jump so that you head the ball when you are at your highest point.

Midfield

Great midfield players are often known as "generals" because of the way their influence extends to every part of the game. Midfielders may be required to help the defence or the attack. They have the freedom to roam in and out of defence or attack whenever needed.

To control a high ball, cushion it on your chest.

BALL CONTROL

Mastery of the ball is crucial. Bringing the ball under control in one movement can give midfield players those extra few seconds, allowing them to pass the ball with pinpoint accuracy.

TRAPPING

One of the main ways to control the ball is trapping. This involves stopping the ball dead between the sole of your foot and the ground. As the ball comes towards you, lift up your foot and let the ball wedge itself under your boot. Keeping your eye on the ball and timing are very important.

Lothar Matthäus for Germany hitting a long pass

LONG PASSES

Knowing when to play a short ball to a nearby colleague or hit a long pass upfield is all part of the midfielder's art. A long or lofted pass can be played by giving yourself a short run up to the ball and approaching it at an angle. To get the height you need, lean back slightly as you are about to strike the ball and hit it at the bottom with your instep.

SHORT PASSES

To hit a short push pass accurately to another player, use the inside part of your foot. Keep the other foot nearby and your eye on the ball. Strike the middle of the ball, keeping it low. The ball will travel in the direction you are facing. Ideally, it should be played just in front of your team mate.

Turn your leg outwards from the hip and use the inside of your foot to push pass.

Trapping the ball is aided by the studs on the sole of your boot.

Practise your dribbling by setting up a row of cones.

Don't kick the ball too far ahead.

Keep the ball close to your foot.

Use the outside of your foot to straighten the ball.

Push the ball forwards a little with the inside of your foot.

DRIBBLING

Watching midfield players run with the ball past opponents is one of the most exciting aspects of football, but it involves a high level of skill. When dribbling, it is important to keep control of the ball so that you can change direction at any time. The ball should be kept in front of you by using gentle taps from either the inside or outside of your foot. If you are confronted by an opponent, push the ball one way and when the player moves in that direction, take the ball the other way to go past him or her.

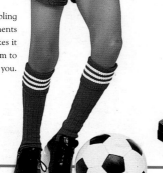

Skilful dribbling confuses opponents and makes it hard for them to tackle you.

Holland's attacker, Dennis Bergkamp, leaps to an immense height, causing aerial chaos among the English defence.

Attacking

Apart from being an accurate header and striker of the ball, to be a good goalscorer, an attacker has to learn how to be in the right place at the right time. He or she has to anticipate passes and crosses and run into position at the right time to catch opponents out.

Diego Maradona loses his Italian opponent, defender Franco Baresi.

ATTACKING HEADERS

In contrast to a defensive header, as an attacker attempting to head the ball into the goal you should firmly head the ball down. This means that you need to get a great deal of spring into your jump in order not only to outleap the defenders, but also to get over the ball as well. Aim your header to bounce close to the goal line so that it is more difficult for the keeper to reach. As with a defensive header, the forehead should be used and it is important to attack the ball with confidence and not just dive in hopefully.

LOSING YOUR MARKER

A great striker will manage to make space for him or herself no matter how tightly he or she is being marked. To do this, it is important to change direction or stop suddenly when making a run in order to confuse the defender. Once you have broken free from your marker, the ball should be played to you quickly before the defender has a chance to catch you. It is important to remember that on average a player has the ball for only three minutes in a game, so a lot of the work has to be done off the ball.

When shooting, don't lean back too far or the ball will go over the bar. To keep the ball low, you must lean over it and kick the top half.

Spread out your arms to help you balance.

Keep your eye on the ball and your opponent as he or she moves in to tackle.

Push the ball one way and when the defender moves in that direction, push the ball away from him or her.

SHOOTING

Whether it is a tap-in, a drive from outside the penalty area, or a volley that almost bursts through the net, if you don't shoot you won't score. A good shot should combine power and accuracy. To do this with the ball on the ground, place your supporting foot close to the ball and using the inside of your shooting foot, take a small backswing and strike the ball cleanly in the middle.

FORMATIONS

WITHIN THE RULES as they stand a team can adopt whatever formation they like. If they wished, they could play with a goalkeeper and ten attackers all charging after the ball. Indeed, the first football games were probably played very much in that way. However, since then the game has developed and over the years various different formations have been employed in order to find that elusive winning formula. Here are some of the most important.

The most effective teams adopt a formation (an arrangement of players) that gives them the best "shape" to carry out the tactics developed by the coach or manager.

The Preston North End team who won the English League and FA Cup in 1889

CLASSIC FORMATION

This formation, with two fullbacks, a right-, centre-, and left-halfback, and five forwards (2-3-5), although very attack-minded, was the first real attempt to play a more defensive system. It was used by England and Scotland in the mid-1880s and, most successfully, by Preston North End when they became the first English side to win the English League and FA Cup "double" in 1889.

The 1927 English FA Cup winners, Arsenal, who used the WM formation

WM FORMATION

In 1925 changes to the offside law gave rise to a massive increase in the number of goals scored. To combat this, English footballer Charlie Buchan of Arsenal and his manager Herbert Chapman developed the WM formation. In this system the centre-halfback was brought back into defence to mark the opposing centre-forward, and both inside-forwards were played just behind the attack in order to create goalscoring chances. Arsenal used this formation very successfully in the 1930s and it became extremely popular the world over.

Charlie Buchan and the Arsenal team. Buchan developed the WM formation with his manager.

Herbert Chapman

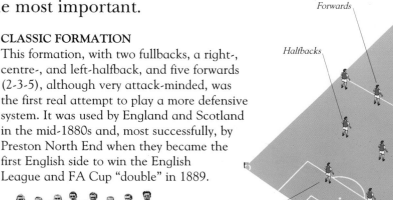

Forwards

Halfbacks

Fullbacks

Attackers span the width of the pitch

CLASSIC 2-3-5 FORMATION

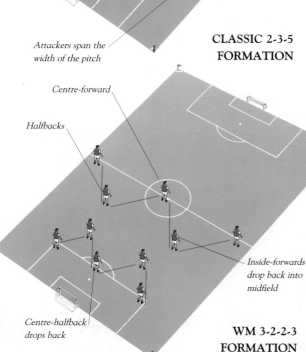

Centre-forward

Halfbacks

Inside-forwards drop back into midfield

Centre-halfback drops back

WM 3-2-2-3 FORMATION

4-2-4 FORMATION AND VARIATIONS

Devised by the great Hungarian team of the early 1950s, the 4-2-4 formation was used to great effect by the 1958 Brazilian World Cup winning side. It was another very attack-minded system. The two fullbacks were expected to push forward, effectively creating a 2-4-4 set-up at times. Later Brazilian teams pulled one of the wingers back into midfield, giving a 4-3-3 formation. The England World Cup winning team of 1966 played a 4-4-2 system, which was more defensive. The fullbacks were not expected to push forward and one of the midfielders played just in front of the back four to act as a defensive screen.

Hungary using the 4-2-4 formation against England in 1953

England playing the 4-4-2 system against Portugal in their 1966 World Cup semifinal

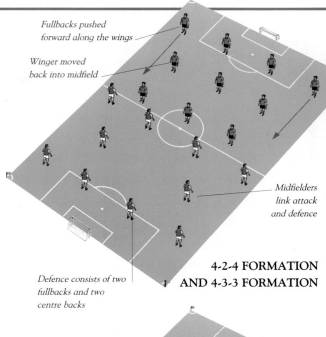

Fullbacks pushed forward along the wings

Winger moved back into midfield

Midfielders link attack and defence

Defence consists of two fullbacks and two centre backs

4-2-4 FORMATION AND 4-3-3 FORMATION

SWEEPER SYSTEM

A sweeper is a defender who moves freely behind the defence. Playing a sweeper behind the back four was originally part of the very defensive "catenaccio" system developed in Italy. The sweeper would roam around behind the defence attempting to catch any attackers who might break through. This system, which was used very effectively by Italian club sides, made it extremely hard for opposing sides to score goals. However, Franz Beckenbauer turned the sweeper's role into a far more attacking one by sometimes playing in front of the back four and, occasionally, bringing the ball forward himself, well into the opponents' half.

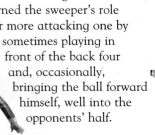

One of the great sweepers, Franz Beckenbauer

Only two forwards

Three midfielders

Back four

Sweeper is the last line of defence

SWEEPER SYSTEM

FORMATIONS TODAY

The 5-3-2 system and the 4-4-2 system are currently vying for predominance. A number of teams are favouring a return to the 4-4-2 system. In reality, the 5-3-2 formation is a system that fluctuates, effectively making a 3-5-2 formation in attacking situations and a 5-3-2 formation in defence.

Every new attacking formation quickly breeds a new defensive system for defeating it. Consequently, it is generally easier to produce effective defensive formations than successful attacking ones.

Italy's Paolo Maldini is one of the most renowned attacking fullbacks.

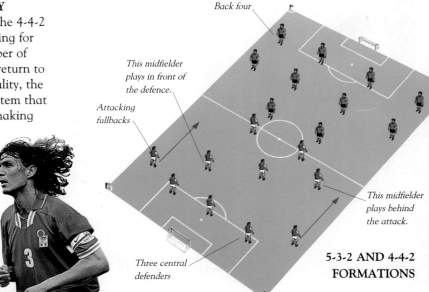

Back four

This midfielder plays in front of the defence.

Attacking fullbacks

This midfielder plays behind the attack.

Three central defenders

5-3-2 AND 4-4-2 FORMATIONS

CHAMPIONSHIPS AND TROPHIES

WINNING THE WORLD CUP is the pinnacle of any player's career, but it would take an awfully long time to fill a trophy cabinet if there was nothing else to play for. Thankfully, throughout the world there are many other championships at both international and club level. Each one is eagerly sought after, for as any player who has ever battled through numerous qualifying matches will confirm, there is no feeling in the world like lifting a trophy in front of thousands of jubilant supporters.

National Team Competitions

Jürgen Klinsmann and his team mates celebrating Germany's victory over the Czech Republic in the 1996 European Championship Final

EUROPEAN CHAMPIONSHIP
The brainchild of Frenchman Henri Delaunay, the European Championship finals have been held every four years since 1960. Over the years, the format has changed and currently it resembles a World Cup for Europe, with teams taking part in a two-year qualifying tournament to earn the right to compete in the final stages. Only the hosts gain automatic entry to the final stages.

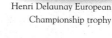

Henri Delaunay European Championship trophy

WORLD CUP FOR WOMEN
The women's World Cup was first held in 1991. Just like the men's World Cup, teams take part in a qualifying tournament to enter the final stages, which are hosted by one nation. Holders and hosts gain automatic entry to the final stages.

The Norway women's team, celebrating their World Cup victory in 1995

Jules Rimet trophy

The original men's World Cup trophy was named after Jules Rimet. Brazil were allowed to keep this trophy after winning the World Cup for a third time in 1970. It was later stolen and melted down for its gold content. The current World Cup trophy was first presented in 1974.

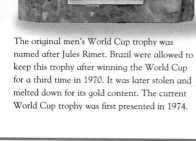

COPA AMERICA (ORIGINALLY CALLED SOUTH AMERICAN CHAMPIONSHIP)

Originally open to the ten members of South America's governing body of football, CONMEBOL, this is the longest running international tournament. First held in 1910, the tournament has been through a number of changes. Since 1993, Mexico and the USA have taken part and the format consists of three groups of four, from which eight proceed to a knockout phase.

Copa America

CENTRAL AMERICAN CHAMPIONSHIP

This championship began in 1941 and is held every two years.

ASIAN CUP AND OCEANIA CUP

The Asian Cup has been running since 1956 and is competed for every four years. The Oceania Cup competition has been held in 1973 and 1980.

Asian Cup

Sergio Martinez of Uruguay lifts the Copa America in 1995.

Asian Cup finalists for the fourth time in a row, Saudi Arabia celebrate their victory in 1996.

European Cup

African Nations Cup

South African goalscorer Mark Williams with the African Nations Cup in 1996

Nigeria's victorious men's team with their Olympic gold medals in 1996

AFRICAN NATIONS CUP

Only Egypt, Ethiopia, and Sudan took part in the first finals of this tournament in 1957, but it has since grown to become a continent-wide competition. Since 1992, 12 teams have competed in the final stages. The hosts and holders automatically qualify for the finals tournament.

OLYMPICS

Football has been an Olympic sport for men since 1908. It has been through a number of changes, mainly due to the original problems of trying to keep it open only to amateurs. The current tournament, for which a worldwide qualifying tournament is played, is for national, professional Under-23 teams. The 1996 Games saw the first women's football tournament to be played at an Olympics.

Club Competitions

Italian team Juventus celebrate their World Club Championship victory in Tokyo in 1996.

World Club Cup

WORLD CLUB CHAMPIONSHIP

The World Club Championship has been played between the winners of the European Cup and the South American Copa Libertadores since 1960. Originally a two-leg home and away tie was used, but since 1980 a single match has been played in Tokyo to decide the Championship.

AFRICAN CLUB COMPETITIONS

There are three main African club competitions. The African Cup of Champion Clubs is open to the League champions of each country and the African Cup Winners' Cup is for the knockout Cup winners from each country. A more recent addition is the CAF Cup for League runners-up.

African Cup of Champion Clubs

Juventus celebrate winning the Italian Serie A in 1996 and qualifying for the European Cup.

EUROPEAN CLUB COMPETITIONS

There are three annual club competitions in Europe. The most prestigious is the European Cup (officially European Champions League), which until recently was competed for by the League champions of each country. It has now been extended to include the League runners-up of the stronger nations. European teams who win their country's knockout Cup competition enter the European Cup Winners' Cup. The UEFA Cup, formerly known as the Fairs Cup, is usually competed for by the top clubs of a country who have not qualified for either of the other two European club events.

Players from Argentinian team River Plate celebrate their Copa Libertadores victory in 1996.

COPA LIBERTADORES

The Copa Libertadores is South America's main club competition. Played annually since 1960, it is the equivalent of the European Cup and is competed for by the League champions of each South American country.

Copa Libertadores

STADIUMS

As LONG AS YOU have a ball, a couple of tin cans for goalposts, and some space, it's possible to play football just about anywhere. However, there are some places where the atmosphere makes the game that little bit special. Some stadiums are almost as famous as the players and clubs that have played there.

MARACANA, RIO DE JANEIRO, BRAZIL

The Maracana, which takes its name from a minor river which runs nearby, is the largest stadium in the world. Its current capacity is 120,000. A world record of 199,854 people turned up at the Maracana to see Brazil face Uruguay in the 1950 World Cup Final. Brazil needed only a draw to become champions, but the majority of the crowd left disappointed as Uruguay won 2-1. The Maracana also holds the attendance record for a club match. This was achieved in 1963 when 177,656 spectators watched a match between Brazilian clubs Flamengo and Fluminense.

The Maracana Stadium opened in 1950, but was not fully completed until 1965.

HAMPDEN PARK, GLASGOW, SCOTLAND

Until the Maracana opened, Hampden Park was the largest stadium in the world. In 1937 149,415 people (a European record) saw Scotland defeat England 3-1, and just seven days later 147,365 spectators crammed in for the Scottish Cup Final between Celtic and Aberdeen. By the mid-1970s, the stadium was in need of repair, and work to convert it into a 50,000 all-seater venue began.

The Azteca Stadium in Mexico during the opening ceremony of the 1986 World Cup

ESTADIO GUILLERMO CAÑEDO, MEXICO CITY MEXICO

Formerly known as the Azteca, this is the only stadium to have played host to two World Cup Finals, in 1970 and 1986. It was built for the 1968 Olympics, but the first game played there was in 1966, when Mexico took on Italian club Torino. With a capacity of 110,000, and a lower tier only ten metres from the pitch, the stadium is famed for its intense atmosphere.

BERNABEU, MADRID, SPAIN

The Bernabeu Stadium, the home of Real Madrid

After the Nuevo Chamartin Stadium was ravaged in Spain's civil war, Real Madrid's president, Santiago Bernabeu, raised 41 million pesetas to build a new one. The 105,000 capacity Bernabeu Stadium stands proudly on Madrid's most prestigious street, Castellana. It opened in 1947 and was made famous by Real Madrid's domination of the European Cup in the 1950s. It has hosted three European Cup Finals as well as the 1982 World Cup Final between Italy and West Germany.

Inside the amazing San Siro Stadium during the 1990 World Cup finals tournament

The Nou Camp Stadium, home to the Barcelona team

NOU CAMP, BARCELONA, SPAIN

Completed in 1957 at a cost of 66 million pesetas, the Nou Camp Stadium has a capacity of 115,000, just big enough to house the 110,000 members who make Barcelona the world's biggest club. However, with work constantly going on, as the club's membership increases, so should capacity. In 1971 an indoor sports hall was opened. There is also a 16,500 capacity mini-stadium across a walkway where Barcelona's nursery team play in the Spanish lower divisions.

SAN SIRO, MILAN, ITALY

Home to Italian clubs AC Milan and Internazionale, the San Siro, or Giuseppe Meazza Stadium, is one of the great wonders of the modern footballing world. From an original capacity of 35,000 in 1926, it has grown considerably. In 1990 eleven cylindrical towers allowed for a third tier and a roof and increased the capacity to 83,000 in time for the World Cup finals tournament. However, this created a problem for the groundstaff as the roof prevents light and rain from reaching the pitch.

WEMBLEY STADIUM, LONDON, ENGLAND

With its twin towers, Wembley Stadium is without doubt the most famous football arena in the world. The legendary Pele called it the church of football and said, "Wembley is the home of the beautiful game." Originally built to be the centre-piece of the British Empire Exhibition in 1924, the stadium was actually completed in 1923 and had a capacity of 127,000. That year it staged the historic FA Cup Final between West Ham and Bolton Wanderers. More than 200,000 people turned up and had to be dispersed by police before the game could begin. As England's national stadium, it now stages all of the English FA Cup Finals.

Today Wembley is an all-seater stadium with a capacity of 80,000. It will soon be undergoing a major face-lift but the twin towers are two features that won't be disappearing.

THE DEVELOPING GAME

AT ONE TIME NO WORLD CUP finals tournament was complete without one of the major national teams inflicting a devastating defeat upon one of the weaker national sides. However, there are no easy games any more. All over the world interest in football is growing among women and men and many national sides are developing rapidly. The future of the game is surely guaranteed.

The number of women involved in both officiating and playing the game is growing.

TALENTED USA PLAYERS

Talented soccer players in the USA are often good all-round athletes who are soon signed up by major baseball, basketball, and American football teams. So although soccer has thrived at college level, until the advent of Major League Soccer in 1996, top players rarely reached professional league level.

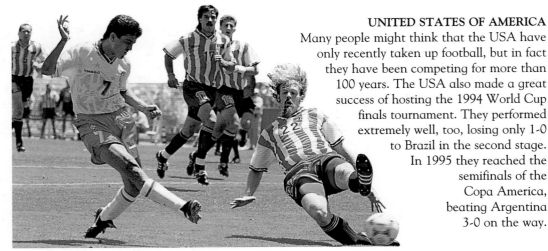

Lalas (above right) is one of the best-known USA players.

UNITED STATES OF AMERICA

Many people might think that the USA have only recently taken up football, but in fact they have been competing for more than 100 years. The USA also made a great success of hosting the 1994 World Cup finals tournament. They performed extremely well, too, losing only 1-0 to Brazil in the second stage. In 1995 they reached the semifinals of the Copa America, beating Argentina 3-0 on the way.

The USA men's team celebrate a victory against England in 1994 in a friendly match. John Harkes holds the trophy.

The opening ceremony of the 1996 Olympic Games in the USA. The attendance figures for the Olympic football tournament were much higher than anticipated, indicating the increasing popularity of the game in the USA.

NEW USA LEAGUE

In 1996 a new outdoor professional league, called Major League Soccer, filled the gap left by the collapse of the North American Soccer League (NASL). As well as overseas stars, the new league has encouraged more home-grown players to become involved. Attendance figures have been good.

Women's football is rapidly gaining recognition. Norway (left) is one of the strongest international teams, shown here in their victorious match against the USA in the women's 1995 World Cup semifinals.

Nigeria celebrate their 3-2 victory over Argentina in the 1996 Olympic Final for Under-23 national sides.

THE WOMEN'S GAME

FIFA's comment that the future of football is feminine is an indication of the rapid growth of the women's game. FIFA now have a women's committee and even though there are currently no professional leagues, Italy's and Japan's are semi-professional and many women players are paid. The women's World Cup was first held in China in 1991 and women's football became an Olympic sport for the first time at Atlanta in 1996. Women's football is also currently the fastest growing sport in Britain and the most popular women's sport in the USA with around eight million participants.

China at the women's Olympic tournament in 1996.

AFRICA

Pele predicted that an African nation would win the World Cup by the year 2000. When Cameroon defeated holders Argentina in the opening game of the 1990 World Cup finals tournament, people began to understand why. Since then African national sides, in particular Nigeria, have continued to impress with their flowing, attacking football. Their success is reflected in African teams being awarded five places at the 1998 World Cup finals tournament, compared with only three places in 1994. At club level the African game suffers from poor administration and facilities, and all the continent's best players join European clubs.

Guido Buchwald and Thomas Berthold for Germany and Sun Hong Hwang for South Korea during the 1994 World Cup finals tournament. South Korea scored two goals against Germany, although they eventually lost 2-3.

The famous opening match in the 1990 World Cup finals tournament when Cameroon won 1-0 against Argentina with a goal by Oman Biyik

ASIA

Half of the world's registered football players are from Asia. Unfortunately, the huge size of the continent makes organizing international competitions difficult. However, with growing economic prosperity in some parts of the region, more money has come into the game in recent years. This has led to growth in the number of professional leagues and more interest from TV companies. Japan's big money J-League has also attracted a number of top foreign players and coaches. Finally, with FIFA awarding the 2002 World Cup to Japan and South Korea jointly, Asian interest in football is bound to rise even more in forthcoming years.

Peng Weiguo for China and Hirochi Nanami and Kazuyoshi Miura for Japan in the 1996 Asian Cup

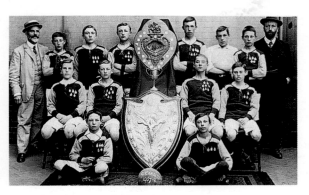
A British youth team, Rucknolt, in 1907

SO YOU WANT TO BECOME A PROFESSIONAL

THERE CAN BE LITTLE DOUBT that being a top professional footballer today has many rewards, not least of which is that you can spend most of your time actually playing the game you love. But those who dream of one day scoring the winning goal in a World Cup Final should be warned. Only very, very few players make it to the top and they have to work extremely hard to get there.

Whether you like to play in goal or as an attacker, there will be specialized techniques to practise and master.

The basic skills of football can be picked up at a very early age.

STEP 1: JOIN UP
There's absolutely no point in dreaming about being a footballer if you don't go out on to a pitch and play the game. So the first thing to do is to join a team. For most young players this will be either a school team or a youth club team that plays in a local league.

Junior players in China prepare for football trials.

STEP 2: BEING SPOTTED

Obviously the next step, that of becoming a good player, depends on a mixture of natural talent and practice. If you do show some potential, you will want to be noticed by a professional club scout. Every club has a scouting system. Some club scouts are looking for established players that the team might want to buy, but others are looking for outstanding players as young as six or seven to take back to the club and develop at a school of excellence. Don't worry if there isn't a club scout in your area. Your teacher or team coach can ask a scout to come and watch you play if he or she thinks that you may be good enough.

Breaking for lunch at a football training school

Starting young with Holland's Ajax Under-12 team

STEP 4: A SCHOOL OF EXCELLENCE

Most of the big professional clubs now have a school of excellence where they develop and train young talent. If you have been successful at a trial, you may be invited to join such a school. However, this is no guarantee of future success, and many young players either drop out or are asked to leave if they cannot cope with the demands.

STEP 3: A TRIAL

Once spotted by a club scout, you will be invited to the club for a trial. As well as finding out how you perform with a ball, the club will be interested in your health, fitness, attitude, and wishes. They will, of course, also speak to your parents.

Club scouts looking for gifted young players may attend local matches.

It takes years of experience to score that goal.

Players at the Ajax training school in Holland

STEP 5: LEARNING A TRADE

Those who do make it through the school of excellence are invited to stay with the club. However, before the glory of scoring that winning goal there are many first team players' boots to be cleaned and kits to be hung up. Yet if you can rise up through the youth, reserve, and nursery teams, maybe your dream of becoming a top footballer will come true.

WHAT DOES EVERYONE DO?

THE STARS OF ANY football match are the players. However, there are many other people involved who ensure those players are fit and healthy, understand what tactics they are supposed to be playing, don't trip over divots on the pitch, and, of course, get paid. Here and on the following pages you can find out about some of these people.

Above, Chelsea coach Dave Sexton uses miniature football to demonstrate tactics to manager Tommy Docherty and the Chelsea players in 1963.

Marcello Lippi, the Juventus Manager, in 1996

THE MANAGER

The manager is the person the players call the boss and it is his or her job to try and create a winning team. The manager decides what to do in training, plans the tactics, motivates the players before a game, decides what new players it might be necessary to buy, and actually picks the team. Almost all managers will have been players themselves, although it is not necessarily the best players who make the best managers.

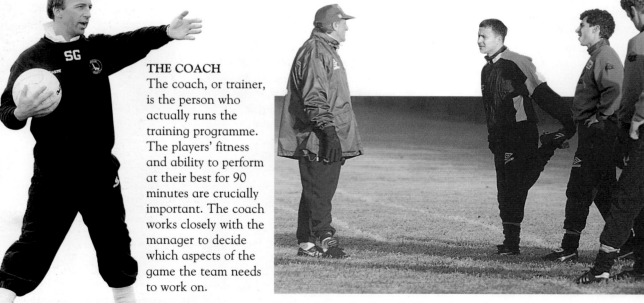

THE COACH

The coach, or trainer, is the person who actually runs the training programme. The players' fitness and ability to perform at their best for 90 minutes are crucially important. The coach works closely with the manager to decide which aspects of the game the team needs to work on.

During training sessions the coach will show the team the lessons they can learn from their previous performances.

THE PHYSIOTHERAPIST

Whenever players are injured during a football match, they will be attended to by a physiotherapist. As well as seeing to the players' needs on the pitch, he or she helps players regain match fitness after broken legs, pulled muscles, sprains, tendon troubles, or cartilage problems. The physiotherapist also checks that players are fit enough to play in a match to ensure that they do not risk serious injury by playing when not fully fit.

During a game, the physiotherapist has to be ready to run on to the pitch at any time to attend to injured players. Above, a physiotherapist uses a spray to alleviate the pain of a leg injury.

Injured players follow a series of exercises specified by the physiotherapist to regain fitness.

Left, Silvio Berlusconi (chairperson) and right, Fabio Capello (coach) celebrate after AC Milan win the Italian League in 1994.

THE CHAIRPERSON

The chairperson, or president, is the head of the whole football club. He or she and a board of directors are responsible for the financial arrangements at the club and work in close consultation with the manager to decide how much money is available to buy new players. Chairpersons are usually business people or celebrities, although very occasionally they are ex-footballers.

Rain stops play! Groundstaff attempt to clear flood waters at Stamford Bridge, England in 1965. Chelsea's game was cancelled.

After each match the team's kit has to be washed and made ready for the next game.

PREPARING THE KIT

The person who organizes the team's kit has to make sure that for every game each player has a full set of clean shirts, shorts, socks, and boots. Sometimes players in a club's youth or reserve side help to get the kit ready.

THE GROUNDSTAFF

At the beginning of the season many football pitches look like smooth green carpets, the grass freshly mown, and not a divot in sight. As the season progresses and more games are played on the surface, it is the job of the groundstaff to make sure that the pitch remains in good condition. A poor pitch results in greater likelihood of injury and second-rate performances. Synthetic surfaces are still relatively rare, especially outside the USA, so the groundstaff's role remains of crucial importance.

Maintenance of the pitch is essential and a team of people is responsible for keeping weeds at bay and limiting the damage caused by the environment and matches. This groundsman is using a hot-air blower to clear the pitch.

8.30 a.m. Groundstaff open up. Pitch inspected.

9.00 a.m. General office and ticket office open.

9.15 a.m. Match programmes delivered.

BEHIND THE SCENES ON MATCH DAY

AS WELL AS THE 22 players, referee, and two assistant referees, behind the scenes a whole army of people is needed to make today's football matches happen. Work starts many hours before the game kicks off and continues well after the game ends and the fans go home. The timetable described here is very generalized, and around the world some things are done slightly differently, but it does give an insight into the preparation involved in putting on a football match for a major club side.

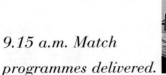

9.30 a.m. Home-team kit laid out.
10.30 a.m. Refreshment stands stocked up.

11.00 a.m. Catering staff begin to prepare meals for sponsors and guests.

12.00 p.m. Match officials arrive. Examine pitch to make sure it is playable.

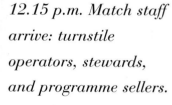

12.15 p.m. Match staff arrive: turnstile operators, stewards, and programme sellers.

12.45 p.m. Police and paramedics arrive. Briefed by stadium manager. Stewards briefed. Closed circuit TV monitoring system switched on.

1.00 p.m. Home-team players arrive.

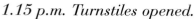

1.15 p.m. Turnstiles opened.

1.45 p.m. Away team arrives.

2.00 p.m. Fans begin to arrive.

2.15 p.m. Teams warm up on pitch then return to dressing rooms.

2.30 p.m. Managers give list of players in teams to referee. Pre-match entertainment begins.

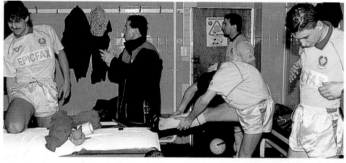

2.45 p.m. Managers give pre-match team talk.

2.55 p.m. Referees lead teams out.

2.55 p.m. Coach, manager, physiotherapist, and substitutes take their places at side of pitch.

3.00 p.m. Match kicks off.

3.45 p.m. Half-time. Groundstaff check pitch.

4.00 p.m. Second half starts.

4.05 p.m. Security firm collects takings.

4.45 p.m. Game ends. Fans begin to leave.

4.50 p.m. TV coverage ends after post-match interviews.

4.55 p.m. Police and stewards debriefed. Groundstaff check pitch.

5.00 p.m. Players bathe. Kits sorted for washing.

5.05 p.m. Catering staff clear up. Rubbish cleared from stands.

5.30 p.m. Teams leave.

5.45 p.m. Match staff leave.

6.30 p.m. Stadium empty. Commercial manager or catering manager locks up.

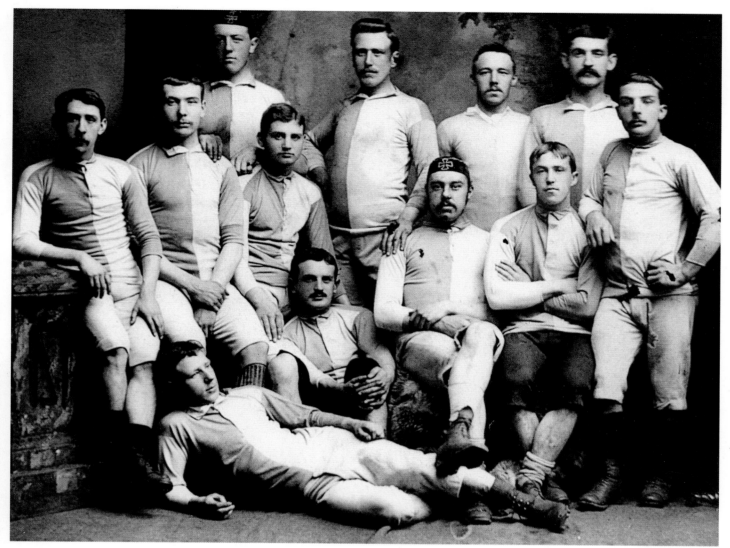

1882 English Cup Final team, Blackburn Rovers

GREAT TEAMS

Football is about eleven people working together like a well-oiled machine. Over the years, there have been many great teams who have produced some dazzling displays of football and won the world's most prestigious trophies along the way.

Note: Team factfiles list the top goalscorers and most capped players for each national side (with years they played), plus a summary of each team's major achievements.

Confederacao Brasileira de Futebol, founded in 1914

BRAZIL

MOST PEOPLE AGREE THAT there has never been a greater football team than the Brazilian World Cup winning side of 1970. Their sublime, flowing football left opponents reeling and football fans around the globe in ecstasy. Although there has never been another side like them, Brazilian teams before and since have always been full of flair and invention. With dazzling displays of ball control and some amazing free kicks, they captivate audiences the world over. Brazil are the 1994 world champions and the most successful international side ever.

Romario holds the World Cup trophy after Brazil's 1994 victory over Italy.

HISTORY

Migrant British workers introduced football to Brazil at the end of the nineteenth century. Due to the size of the country, it wasn't until 1971 that a national League was set up.

Brazil has produced some of the world's greatest players, such as

Djalma Santos, Garrincha, Pele, Jairzinho, Romario, and Ronaldo to

name but a few. Their brilliant dribbling and

"awesome finishing"

have brought joy to millions.

Brazil with the Swedish flag after winning the World Cup in 1958 against Sweden in Stockholm

AN UNPARALLELED SUCCESS

Brazil are the only national side to have played in every World Cup. They have won the tournament a record four times in 1958, 1962, 1970, and 1994. They were runners-up to Uruguay in 1950, and were third-placed in 1938 and 1978. Brazil have also won the South American Championship on five occasions.

WINNING IN 1994

The key to Brazil's 1994 World Cup success was the partnership of Romario and Bebeto. Romario either scored or helped to create 10 of the 11 goals Brazil gained on their way to the Final. The Final itself ended goalless, and Brazil became the first side to win the World Cup on a penalty shoot-out.

A Brazilian was the first person to win the World Cup as a player (in 1958 and 1962) and then as a manager eight years later. Who was he? (Answers to team questions on page 96)

Brazil's team colours: yellow shirts, blue shorts, and blue socks

PELE
The greatest player ever to pull on a Brazil shirt was Pele, who made his debut for Brazil in 1957 at the age of 16 in a match against Argentina.

Factfile

Top Goalscorers
1. Pele 77 (1957-71)
2. Zico 54 (1971-86)
3. Jairzinho 38 (1963-82)

Most Appearances
1. Djalma Santos 100 (1952-68)
2. Gilmar 95 (1953-69)
3. Roberto Rivelino 94 (1965-78)

1958 World Cup
Brazil beat Sweden 5-2 in the Final.

1962 World Cup
Brazil defeated Czechoslovakia 3-1 in the Final.

1970 World Cup
Brazil beat Italy 4-1 in the Final.

1994 World Cup
Brazil and Italy drew 0-0 in the Final. Brazil won 3-2 on penalties.

Brazil's Ronaldo playing for Barcelona in 1996

PLAYING TO THE BEAT OF A DRUM
Brazilians are among the most colourful and enthusiastic football fans in the world. The whistles and rhythm of samba drums create a party atmosphere when the national side or top club sides, such as Santos, Flamengo, Fluminense, São Paulo, and Vasco da Gama, take to the field.

GARRINCHA
Known as "Little Bird", Garrincha played in both the 1958 and 1962 World Cup winning teams. His skilful footwork destroyed many a defence as England found in the 1962 finals tournament when he scored twice against them.

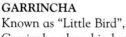

RONALDO
Ronaldo is perhaps the world's most exciting player today. In 1997 aged 20, the Brazilian striker scored the winning goal in Barcelona's European Cup Winners' Cup victory over Paris Saint-Germain.

In 1997 Brazil won the Copa America for the fifth time. Who did they beat in the Final?

GERMANY

Deutscher Fussball-Bund, founded in 1900

Germany's team colours: white shirts, black shorts, and white socks

GERMANY IS BY FAR Europe's most successful footballing nation. The German side have reached the World Cup Final six times, more than any other team, and have won on three occasions. In 1996 Germany became European champions for the third time. With the legendary Franz Beckenbauer and the great goalscorer Gerd Müller, German club side Bayern Munich dominated European football in the 1970s. German reunification in 1990 gave the national side a greater pool of players.

HISTORY

Football began in Germany in the 1880s. By 1898 regional leagues had been set up with the winners of each league competing to be national champions. Post-war Germany was split into East and West, and in 1963 a single national League, the Bundesliga, was formed in West Germany.

WOLFGANG OVERATH

Overath was a midfielder and played all his domestic games with the West German club Köln. He had a key role in the West German World Cup teams of 1966, 1970, and 1974.

Overath (left) and Müller (right) celebrate W. Germany's 2-1 victory over Holland in the 1974 World Cup Final.

"Tactical and determined"

German teams can play a very quick and exciting passing game. They also possess extremely skilful players.

WORLD CHAMPIONS ...

West Germany first won the World Cup in 1954, beating Hungary 3-2 after being two goals down. They won again in 1974, defeating Holland 2-1, and in 1990, beating Argentina 1-0. They were runners-up to England in 1966, losing 4-2, to Italy in 1982, losing 3-1, and to Argentina in 1986, losing 3-2.

... AND EUROPEAN CHAMPIONS!

Germany are the only team to have won the European Championship more than once. They are the 1996 holders, having beaten the Czech Republic 2-1, and they previously defeated Belgium 2-1 in 1980 and the Soviet Union 3-0 in 1972.

 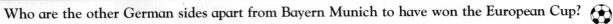

GERD MÜLLER

Known as "Der Bomber", Gerd Müller (right) was lethal in front of goal. He is Germany's highest goalscorer of all time, with a staggering 68 goals in 62 internationals. He also scored 365 times in the German League for Bayern Munich, a record which still stands today.

Factfile

(Including W. Germany)

Top Goalscorers
1. Gerd Müller 68 (1966-74)
2. Rudi Völler 47 (1982-94)
3. Karl-Heinz Rummenigge 45 (1976-86)

Most Appearances
1. Lothar Matthäus 122 (1980-94)
2. Franz Beckenbauer 103 (1965-77)
3. Jürgen Klinsmann 100 (1987-)

Müller (above) was a powerful centre-forward with great heading ability and a remarkable goal-scoring talent.

1974 World Cup
W. Germany beat Holland 2-1 in the Final.

1990 World Cup
W. Germany defeated Argentina 1-0 in the Final.

1996 European Championship
Germany beat the Czech Republic 2-1 in the Final.

BAYERN MUNICH

With 14 League titles to their name and European Cup wins in 1974, 1975, and 1976, Bayern Munich are Germany's most successful club side. With Beckenbauer as manager, they also won the UEFA Cup in 1996.

JÜRGEN KLINSMANN

Loved by fans wherever he goes, Jürgen Klinsmann lifted the 1996 European Championship trophy as captain of his country. A prolific goalscorer, he scored 15 goals in Bayern Munich's 1996 UEFA Cup campaign – a record for goals scored in a single European club competition.

Jürgen Klinsmann in action in the European Championship in 1996. He is one of Germany's greatest strikers, and scored three goals during the championship.

FRANZ BECKENBAUER

One of the world's greatest players, Beckenbauer captained West Germany to World Cup glory in 1974 and was their winning manager in the 1990 World Cup.

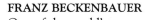

Who was the last German to miss a penalty in a penalty shoot-out in any game?

ITALY

AT INTERNATIONAL LEVEL, Italy have appeared in five World Cup Finals, winning three times, and have won the European Championship once, in 1968. Without doubt Italians play some of the best football in the world, but in the past they were criticised for playing too defensively. The top league division in Italy, Serie A, is generally regarded as the best in the world, with many of the world's biggest stars, huge attendances, and skilful, exciting matches. Italian club sides, notably Juventus and AC Milan, have won many European titles.

Federazione Italiana Giuoco Calcio, founded in 1898

Italy's team colours: blue shirts, white shorts, and blue socks

HISTORY
The first Italian League champions were Genoa in 1898. However, they only had to play three games to win the title. It wasn't until 1929 that a single national league was introduced and the number of games played greatly increased.

PAOLO ROSSI
A star of the 1978 World Cup, Rossi was the top scorer in the 1982 World Cup with six goals, including the first goal against West Germany.

PAOLO MALDINI
Considered to be the best defender in the world, Maldini is the most capped player of the current Italian squad.

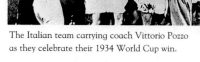

The Italian team carrying coach Vittorio Pozzo as they celebrate their 1934 World Cup win.

THE GLORY YEARS
The 1930s were the greatest years for Italian football. In this entire decade, Italy lost only nine games. The acclaimed coach, Vittorio Pozzo, led them to victory in the World Cup in 1934 and 1938, and at the Olympics in 1936. Their post-war success included winning the European Championship in 1968 and the World Cup for a third time in 1982.

Zoff raising the World Cup trophy in 1982

DINO ZOFF
The legendary goalkeeper Zoff became the oldest player to lift the World Cup when he captained the winning side of 1982 aged 40. He went on to manage top Italian sides Juventus and Lazio.

  Which team shocked the world by beating Italy 1-0 in the World Cup finals of 1966?

Marco Tardelli scores against W. Germany in the 1982 World Cup Final.

UNDER PRESSURE

Italy's players often seem under greater pressure to succeed than any others. But when they do experience victory, their joy is unbridled. Above, Marco Tardelli expresses his elation on scoring Italy's second goal in the 1982 World Cup Final.

Italian football can be both exhilarating and frustrating, but at its best it is

"creative and penetrating".

Pietro Vierchowod for Juventus and George Weah for AC Milan in 1996

JUVENTUS AND AC MILAN

The most successful Italian clubs are Juventus of Turin and AC Milan. Between them they have won 13 major European trophies and have topped Serie A 39 times.

CATENACCIO

If you don't concede a goal you can't lose became the philosophy of Italian football in the 1960s and 1970s. Tight defending was the order of the day and free-flowing football suffered. Thankfully, more recently all that has changed as shown by Arrigo Sacchi's breathtaking Milan side of the late 1980s and early 1990s.

FRANCO BARESI

The hard man of Italian football, Baresi was both a solid defender and a very skilful player. Throughout his domestic career, he played for club side AC Milan, with whom he clocked up more than 600 appearances.

AC Milan fans at the 1989 European Cup Final

FERVENT FANS

Italian supporters are some of the most passionate in football. Their constant chanting and firing of colourful flares ensures that the atmosphere in Italian games rarely drops below boiling point.

Factfile

Top Goalscorers
1. Luigi Riva 35 (1965-74)
2. Giuseppe Meazza 33 (1930-39)
3. Silvio Piola 30 (1935-52)

Most Appearances
1. Dino Zoff 112 (1968-83)
2. Giacinto Facchetti 94 (1963-77)
3. Marco Tardelli 81 (1976-85)
   Franco Baresi 81 (1982-94)

1934 World Cup
Italy beat Czechoslovakia 2-1 in the Final.

1938 World Cup
Italy defeated Hungary 4-2 in the Final.

1968 European Championship
Italy beat Yugoslavia 2-0 to become European Champions.

1982 World Cup
Italy defeated W. Germany 3-1 in the Final.

 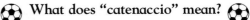

Asociacion del Futbol Argentino, founded in 1893

ARGENTINA

ALONGSIDE BRAZIL, ARGENTINA are the other South American giants of world football. Their most renowned player is the legendary Diego Maradona. He led Argentina to their second World Cup victory in 1986. They first won in 1978. They have reached the Final of four World Cups in total and have won the South American Championship (Copa America) no less than 14 times.

Argentina's team colours: sky blue-and-white striped shirts, black shorts, and white socks

HISTORY

Argentina is the second oldest footballing nation after Britain and was introduced to the game by Britain in 1865. In 1901 Argentina played in the first international match to be held outside Britain. It was against Uruguay, who were to become their arch rivals.

DIEGO MARADONA

Diego Armando Maradona (left) was one of the greatest players the world has ever seen. Though not always on his best behaviour, when the only thing on his mind was football, he was breathtaking.

In 1993 Argentina defeated first time entrants Mexico in the Copa America to become champions for the fourteenth time.

Osvaldo Ardiles

Argentina's style is very much in the

Latin mould, with the emphasis on skilful

"attack-minded play".

WORLD CUP WINS

It was second time lucky for Argentina in 1978 when, after losing the 1930 Final 4-2 to Uruguay, they won the World Cup on home soil, beating Holland 3-1. Eight years later in Mexico, they were champions again after defeating West Germany 3-2. They narrowly missed holding on to the trophy in 1990, losing 1-0 to West Germany.

OSVALDO ARDILES

A tricky attacking midfielder, Ardiles was one of Argentina's most successful exports. After helping his country win the 1978 World Cup, he was transferred to English club Tottenham Hotspur for £300,000.

Argentina and Uruguay have played each other more times than any other two countries. What was the score when they first met in 1901?

RIVER PLATE
The year 1986 was to go down in history for Argentina's most successful club side River Plate. They won the Argentinian League, the Inter-American Cup, the Copa Libertadores, and the World Club Cup.

Zamora for River Plate in the white shirt with red stripe.

1978 World Cup
Argentina beat Holland 3-1 in the Final.

1986 World Cup
Argentina defeated W. Germany 3-2 in the Final.

Striker Mario Kempes played in three World Cups: 1974, 1978, and 1982.

MARIO KEMPES
As an aggressive young striker, Mario Kempes got his first taste of World Cup football in the 1974 tournament. Top scorer of the 1978 World Cup with six goals, Kempes scored two of those in the Final itself, making him the most recent player to score more than one goal in a World Cup Final. Kempes also appeared in the 1982 finals tournament, but his form of 1978 was never recaptured.

Argentina against Uruguay in 1986

THE OLD ENEMY
Argentina's greatest rivals are Uruguay. The two South American sides have faced each other 182 times, making this game the most played international match in the world.

Who did Argentina beat in their semifinal in the first ever World Cup in 1930?

FRANCE

France's team colours: blue shirts, white shorts, and red socks

Fédération Française de Football, founded in 1918

WORLD FOOTBALL OWES a huge debt of gratitude to the French, for it was they who first came up with the idea of a World Cup competition. Sadly, they have never been champions themselves, though they have been semifinalists on three occasions, and Frenchman Just Fontaine holds the record for the number of goals scored in a World Cup finals tournament. France tasted success in 1984 when a side packed with stars, such as the great Platini, Giresse, Tigana, and Battiston, won the European Championship.

France celebrating Platini's goal in the 1984 European Championship Final

HISTORY
Rugby was by far the most popular French sport in the latter half of the last century, and initially, football clubs were offshoots of rugby clubs. It wasn't until 1892 that the first French clubs devoted entirely to football were formed.

Just Fontaine

At their best France play exciting, *"flowing football"*, as epitomized by the 1984 team who won the European Championship and were a joy to watch.

JUST FONTAINE
Fontaine had played just five times for France before the 1958 World Cup finals. Yet he scored in every one of France's matches. He scored 13 goals, more than anyone has ever scored in one tournament.

DEFEAT IN 1982
In the 1982 World Cup semifinal, a dubious challenge by German goalkeeper Harald Schumacher on defender Battiston went unpunished. It was widely seen as a terrible miscarriage of justice. The French battled hard and at the end of extra time the score was 3-3, but they eventually lost on penalties.

Platini scored in every game of the 1984 European Championship. In the Final, who scored France's other goal in their 2-0 victory against Spain?

VICTORY IN 1984

With the brilliant Michel Platini as captain, France won every game en route to beating Spain 2-0 in the 1984 European Championship Final. Playing in midfield, Michel Platini was a genius with a knack for scoring great goals. Lifting the trophy for his country in 1984 was his crowning glory.

Eric Cantona playing for France

ERIC CANTONA

In his six seasons in the English Premier League, Eric Cantona was a championship winner five times. An attacking midfielder for Manchester United and a dominating presence within the team, his skill and vision were second to none. He gave up football in 1997 to pursue a career in acting.

Marcel Desailly playing for France in 1995

Michel Platini playing for France in 1984

JEAN PIERRE PAPIN

A natural goalscorer at both club and national level, Papin has always been a danger to his opponents.

Papin (left) has played for France 54 times. At club level he has played in France, Germany, and Italy.

YOURI DJORKAEFF

One of the new and exciting French players, Djorkaeff's attacking runs and goalscoring ability made him one of his country's stars in the 1996 European Championship.

MARCEL DESAILLY

A hugely talented defender, Desailly (above) was very influential in helping France to reach the semifinals of the European Championship in 1996. He won a European Cup medal with club side Olympique Marseille in 1993, and the following year he won another playing for AC Milan.

Factfile

Top Goalscorers
1. Michel Platini 41 (1976-87)
2. Jean-Pierre Papin 30 (1986-)
3. Just Fontaine 27 (1956-60)

Most Appearances
1. Manuel Amoros 82 (1982-92)
2. Maxime Bossis 76 (1976-86)
3. Michel Platini 72 (1976-87)

1958 World Cup
France were knocked out by Brazil 5-2 in the semifinals.

1982 World Cup
France drew 3-3 with W. Germany in the semifinals after extra time, but lost 5-4 on penalties.

1984 European Championship
France beat Spain 2-0 in the Final.

1986 World Cup
France were beaten by W. Germany 2-0 in the semifinals.

France appeared in the first ever World Cup finals in Uruguay in 1930. Who did they beat 4-1 in their first match?

43

Koninklijke Nederlandsche Voetbalbond, founded in 1889

HOLLAND

HOLLAND ARE PROBABLY the greatest team never to have been crowned world champions. The national side reached the semifinals of four consecutive Olympics: 1908, 1912, 1920, and 1924. In the mid-1970s they reached two World Cup Finals, narrowly losing on both occasions. In 1988, Holland finally won a major title, the European Championship.

Holland's team colours: orange shirt, white shorts, and orange socks

HISTORY

Formed in 1889, the Dutch FA is the third oldest in Europe. The national League however, was formed comparatively late in 1957, when professionalism was introduced.

1988 European Championship side

Ruud Gullit scored the opening goal in the 1988 European Championship Final

RUUD GULLIT

With his distinctive hairstyle and magnificent skills, Ruud Gullit stood out on the football pitch in more ways than one. In 1988 he lifted the European Championship trophy as captain of Holland.

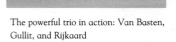

The powerful trio in action: Van Basten, Gullit, and Rijkaard

TOP SIDES

Dutch clubs have always had great success in nurturing the talents of young footballers. This is one reason why clubs such as PSV Eindhoven, Ajax, and Feyenoord have done so well in European competitions. Ajax, for example, produced Johan Cruyff, Dennis Bergkamp, Marco Van Basten, and Frank Rijkaard – four of Holland's all-time greats.

 Who scored Holland's second goal when they won the 1988 European Championship Final?

THOSE WORLD CUPS

On the way to their 2-1 defeat in the 1974 World Cup Final, Holland scored 14 goals and conceded only one. In the Final, Neeskens for Holland scored from the penalty spot before any of the West German players had touched the ball. It was the fastest goal ever in a World Cup Final. In the 1978 Final, the Dutch managed to force the game into extra time before they were defeated by Argentina.

Holland's new style of football in the 1974 World Cup had a profound effect, as every outfield player could function in any position. This style of play became known as **"*total football*".**

Cruyff brought down by Hoeness for a penalty in the 1974 World Cup Final

JOHAN CRUYFF

Cruyff's great ball skills could single-handedly unlock an opponent's defence. He captained Holland in the 1974 World Cup finals and won three European Cups with Ajax.

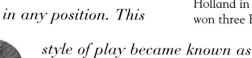

Dennis Bergkamp in the 1994 World Cup

EUROPEAN CHAMPIONS

The 1988 European Championship gave Holland the trophy they deserved. In Ruud Gullit, Frank Rijkaard, and Marco Van Basten, a new set of Dutch stars emerged. By beating West Germany 2-1 in the semifinals, Holland also found consolation for the defeat in the 1974 World Cup Final.

MARCO VAN BASTEN

After scoring 128 league goals for Ajax, in 1987 Marco Van Basten joined Italian club AC Milan, with whom he won the European Cup in 1989 and 1990. He was at his peak during the 1988 European Championship. An ankle injury spoilt the later years of Van Basten's career.

Van Basten in the 1990 World Cup

DENNIS BERGKAMP

Bergkamp (left) is known as the "Ice Man" because of his cool temperament and composed, clinical playing style. He has made more than 40 appearances for his country and scored more than 20 international goals.

 Who were the first Dutch club to win the European Cup?

The English Football Association, founded in 1863

HISTORY

In 1848 Cambridge University drew up the first rules for football. In 1863 the newly formed English Football Association established an agreed set of rules. The English FA Cup began in 1872 and became crucial to the game's development in England.

Leading English players in 1881

WORLD CHAMPIONS IN 1966

Three goals by Geoff Hurst (below, second from left) ensured England's finest hour when they defeated West Germany 4-2 at Wembley Stadium to win the 1966 World Cup. Geoff Hurst is the only player to score a hat trick in a World Cup Final.

ENGLAND

England's team colours: white shirts, blue shorts, and white socks

THE GAME AS WE KNOW IT today has been played in England longer than anywhere else. Probably for that reason, the English have often considered themselves to be the best in the world. Whilst their performances have rarely justified that claim, when they won the World Cup on home soil in 1966, few could argue with it. The English Premier League is widely regarded as the hardest in the world to win, and, with the current influx of foreign superstars, it can also lay claim to being one of the world's most prestigious championships. Club sides such as Manchester United, Liverpool, and Chelsea are famous around the world, and over the years, England has produced some great players, such as Stanley Matthews, Bobby Charlton, Bobby Moore, Alan Shearer, and Paul Gascoigne.

Bobby Moore celebrating England's World Cup win in 1966

TWO GREAT BOBBIES

Bobby Moore captained England to World Cup victory in 1966 and is probably the greatest defender the country has ever produced. In the same victorious side was Bobby Charlton, who has scored more goals for England than anyone else.

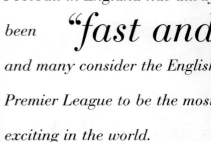

Bobby Charlton

Football in England has alway been **"fast and** *and many consider the English Premier League to be the most exciting in the world.*

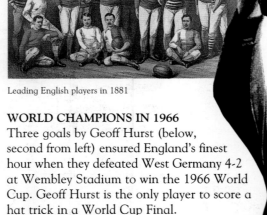

What was the final score of the first ever international match between England and Scotland?

TOP ENGLISH CLUBS

Manchester United became the first English side to win the European Cup in 1968 and more recently they became the only team to win the English League and Cup "double" twice. Liverpool are the most successful club in English football with 18 championship wins, four European Cup victories, and two UEFA Cup triumphs.

Peter Schmeichel and Ole Gunnar Solskjaer for Manchester United against Stan Collymore for Liverpool in 1997

David Seaman saves Nadal's penalty in a 1996 European Championship quarter final against Spain. England won in a penalty shoot-out.

GREAT GOALKEEPERS

England has always produced very fine goalkeepers. In Gordon Banks the England team probably had the best goalkeeper ever and Peter Shilton (below) is their most capped player. David Seaman (above) is regarded by some as the best keeper in the world at the moment.

Factfile

Top Goalscorers
1. Bobby Charlton 49 (1958-70)
2. Gary Lineker 48 (1984-92)
3. Jimmy Greaves 44 (1959-67)

Most Appearances
1. Peter Shilton 125 (1970-90)
2. Bobby Moore 108 (1962-73)
3. Bobby Charlton 106 (1958-70)

1966 World Cup
England defeated W. Germany 4-2 in the Final.

1990 World Cup
England were beaten 4-3 on penalties in the semifinals by W. Germany.

1997 Tournoi de France
England won this four-nation contest on points.

ALAN SHEARER

Alan Shearer became the world's most expensive player when Newcastle paid Blackburn Rovers £15 million for him in 1996. A prolific goalscorer, he is the first man to have scored 100 goals in the English Premier League and he was the top scorer in the 1996 European Championship tournament with five goals.

physical"

Alan Shearer in a first stage group match against Holland in the 1996 European Championship. England won 4-1.

Peter Shilton (above) playing for England in 1989

PAUL GASCOIGNE

Possessing excellent close ball control, superb long-range passing skills, and an ability to conjure up scoring opportunities, Paul Gascoigne is the most gifted English player of his generation. He was outstanding during the 1990 World Cup and was a key player in the 1996 European Championship.

A booking for Gascoigne in the 1990 World Cup semifinals meant that, had England won the game, he would not have been able to play in the Final.

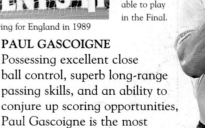

⚽ Which player scored England's fastest ever World Cup goal when he opened their account against ⚽ France in 1982 after just 27 seconds?

47

URUGUAY

Asociacion Uruguaya de Futbol, founded in 1900

PENAROL
Uruguay's most successful club are Penarol. In 1982 they became the first team to win the World Club Cup three times, beating English side Aston Villa 2-0.

WITH THEIR NATIONAL SIDE as Olympic champions, Uruguay hosted the first World Cup in 1930 and, to the delight of the home crowd, they won the trophy. They won the trophy again in 1950, this time in Brazil, becoming the first South American team to win two World Cups. Although the national side have not been in the World Cup reckoning in recent years, they have won the South American Championship 14 times – a record matched only by Argentina.

Uruguay's team colours: blue shirts, black shorts, and black socks

Factfile

Top Goalscorers
1. Hector Scarone 29 (1917-30)
2. Angel Romano 28 (1911-27)
3. Omar Miguez 26 (1950-58)

Most Appearances
1. Rodolfo Rodriguez 78 (1976-86)
2. Enzo Francescoli 70 (1983-97)
3. Angel Romano 69 (1911-27)

1924 Olympics
Uruguay beat Switzerland 3-0 in the Final.

1928 Olympics
Uruguay drew 1-1 in the Final against Argentina, and then won the replay 2-1.

1930 World Cup
Hosts Uruguay defeated Argentina 4-2 in the Final.

The 1928 Olympic Games Final was a 1-1 draw. Uruguay won the replay.

OLYMPIC CHAMPIONS
South American footballers entered the Olympic Games for the first time in 1924. Uruguay defeated Switzerland 3-0 in the Final. Uruguay won the gold medal again in Holland in 1928, defeating Holland, Germany, and Italy, before finally beating their great rivals, Argentina 2-1.

Uruguay's captain (left) and Argentina's captain (right) with the referee and linesmen in the 1928 Olympics.

Lorenzo Fernandez, Pedro Cea, and Hector Scarone celebrate Uruguay's victory in the first World Cup Final in 1930.

Uruguay's goalkeeper, Maspoli, failed to save this shot by Brazil's Friaca in the 1950 World Cup Final. However, Uruguay went on to win 2-1.

WORLD CHAMPIONS
In the first World Cup Final in 1930, hosts Uruguay defeated Argentina 4-2 in front of 93,000 people in Montevideo. In 1950 in Brazil, they shocked local support when they defeated a much-fancied home side 2-1 to become world champions for a second time.

1950 World Cup
Uruguay beat hosts Brazil 2-1 in the Final.

 Who was the captain of Uruguay and the first man to lift the World Cup trophy in 1930?

HUNGARY

Magyar Labdarugo Szovetseg, founded 1901

Hungary's team colours: red shirts, white shorts, and green socks

BETWEEN MAY 1950 AND JULY 1954, Hungary lost only one match. Unfortunately, that was the 1954 World Cup Final. There is no doubt however, that the 1954 Hungarian side were one of the greatest teams of all time. They were known as the "Magical Magyars" and in Ferenc Puskas and Sandor Kocsis they had a deadly striking partnership. Hungary were Olympic champions in 1952, 1964, and 1968, and in 1953 they became the first foreign side to beat England on English soil.

Hungary line up before the match against England at Wembley in 1953.

OLYMPIC CHAMPIONS
Hungary have been Olympic champions three times. Interestingly, on each occasion they have defeated fellow East European teams to take the gold medal, beating Yugoslavia 2-0 in 1952, Czechoslovakia 2-1 in 1964, and Bulgaria 4-1 in 1968.

The captains of each winning side with their medals at the 1964 Olympics. Hungary won gold, Czechoslovakia silver, and West Germany bronze.

WORLD RUNNERS-UP
After beating West Germany 8-3 in a group match, Hungary were confident of winning when the two teams met in the 1954 World Cup Final. Incredibly, Hungary squandered a two-goal lead and allowed the Germans to win 3-2.

W. Germany scoring their first goal against Hungary in the 1954 World Cup Final

Hungary beating Brazil 4-2 in a World Cup quarter final in 1954

Factfile

Top Goalscorers
1. Ferenc Puskas 82 (1945-56)
2. Sandor Kocsis 75 (1948-56)
3. Imre Schlosser 58 (1906-27)

Most Appearances
1. Jozsef Bozsik 100 (1947-62)
2. Laszlo Fazekas 92 (1968-83)
3. Gyula Grosics 86 (1947-62)

1952 Olympics
Hungary defeated Yugoslavia 2-0 in the Final.

1954 World Cup
Hungary were defeated 3-2 in the Final by W. Germany.

1964 Olympics
Hungary defeated Czechoslovakia 2-1 in the Final. They won the Olympics again in 1968 beating Bulgaria 4-1 in the Final.

FERENC PUSKAS
One of the world's greatest footballers, Puskas, who had a deadly left foot, is still Hungary's top goalscorer. Puskas was Hungary's captain and later was able to play for Spain due to residency there.

Puskas playing for Hungary in 1953

All Russian Football Union,
founded in 1912

RUSSIA

RUSSIA, FORMERLY KNOWN as the Soviet Union, has always fielded strong sides that are difficult to beat. In 1956 the Soviets became Olympic champions for the first time and four years later they were the first winners of the European Championship. On both occasions, the legendary Lev Yashin was in goal. They have also reached three other European Championship Finals, finishing as runners-up each time, and in 1988 they again won Olympic gold. World Cup glory however, has eluded them and a semifinal appearance in 1966 has been their best performance.

Russia's team colours: white shirts, blue shorts, and red socks

1960 European champions

EUROPEAN FINALISTS
After winning the first European Championship in 1960, the Soviets lost 2-1 to Spain in the 1964 Final. They also lost 3-0 to West Germany in the 1972 Final, and 2-0 to Holland in the Final of the 1988 championship.

Lev Yashin making a save in the 1956 Olympic Final

LEV YASHIN
Considered by many to be the greatest goalkeeper ever, Yashin played 78 times for his country in a career that ran from 1954 to 1970. Yashin was famous for stopping shots that no other goalkeeper could reach.

Brazil's Farias and Souza clash with Ketachvili of the Soviet Union in the 1988 Olympic Final.

OLYMPIC CHAMPIONS
In front of 120,000 at the Melbourne Cricket Ground, the Soviets beat Yugoslavia to become champions at the 1956 Melbourne Olympics. In 1988 they won gold again at the Seoul Olympics, this time beating Brazil 2-1 in the Final.

The Soviet Union at the 1962 World Cup finals tournament in Chile. They were defeated 2-1 by Chile in the quarter finals.

Apart from Lev Yashin, who is the only other Soviet Union player who has been named European Footballer of the Year?

SPAIN

Spain's team colours: red shirts, blue shorts, and blue socks

Real Federation Española de Futbol, founded in 1913

The triumphant Spanish team with their manager, Villalonga, in 1964

EUROPEAN CHAMPIONS

Spain won the European Championship in 1964 by beating the Soviet Union 2-1 in front of 105,000 people in Madrid's Bernabeu Stadium. Their two goals came from Pereda and Marcelino.

Luis Suarez as a player in 1961 (above) and as the manager of Spain in 1990 (left)

LUIS SUAREZ

Suarez is probably the greatest Spanish footballer of all time. His success came in the 1960s with club side Internazionale of Italy. He went on to be a coach and a manager, and took Spain to the 1990 World Cup.

IN REAL MADRID and Barcelona, Spain has two of the greatest club sides in the world. Between them they have appeared in 27 European competition Finals, winning on 16 occasions. The national side, however, have found success harder to come by. Their only major trophy has been the European Championship in 1964 and they have never reached a World Cup semifinal. More recently, the Under-23 side won the 1992 Olympic tournament. But with the passion the Spanish have for the game, they will always be a force to be reckoned with.

The victorious Under-23 1992 Olympic team

OLYMPIC CHAMPIONS

Once again on home soil, this time in Barcelona's Nou Camp Stadium in front of 95,000 people, Spain's talented young side won the 1992 Olympics by defeating Poland 3-2.

REAL MADRID AND BARCELONA

Fierce rivals, these two teams have dominated the Spanish domestic game for years. In particular, the Real Madrid side of the late 1950s, which won the first five European Cup competitions and boasted such great players as Di Stefano and Puskas, will be remembered as one of the greatest teams ever. More recently however, European success has largely eluded Real Madrid, and Barcelona have been the more successful of the two teams.

Real Madrid in 1960 with Alfredo Di Stefano (holding ball) and Ferenc Puskas (front row, second from right)

Zamorano for Real Madrid (left) and Koeman for Barcelona (right) in 1992

Factfile

Top Goalscorers
1. Emilio Butragueño 26 (1984-92)
2. Alfredo Di Stefano 23 (1957-61)
3. Miguel Gonzalez 'Michel' 21 (1985-93)
   Julio Salinas 21 (1986-96)

Most Appearances
1. Andoni Zubizarreta 110 (1983-)
2. Jose Antonio Camacho 81 (1975-88)
3. Rafael Gordillo 75 (1978-88)

1964 European Championship
Spain beat the Soviet Union 2-1 in the Final.

1992 Olympics
Spain defeated Poland 3-2 in the Final.

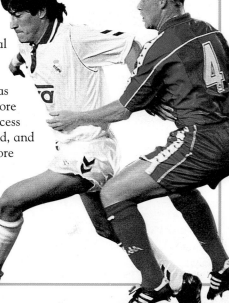

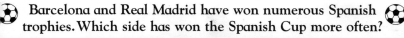

Barcelona and Real Madrid have won numerous Spanish trophies. Which side has won the Spanish Cup more often?

United States Soccer Federation, founded in 1913

USA WOMEN

Winners of the first ever World Cup for women and the 1996 Olympic champions, there is little doubt that the United States women's team are going to be a major side for many years to come. The game in America is being played by more women than ever before and in Michelle Akers they possess the first true star of the women's game.

USA women's team colours: navy shirts, navy shorts, and navy socks (also play in white)

Michelle Akers celebrates Olympic victory in 1996.

Akers clashes with Haugen in 1996.

WORLD CHAMPIONS
The United States won all their games on the way to winning the inaugural women's World Cup in China in 1991. In the Final in Guangzhoa, they defeated Norway 2-1.

SEMIFINALISTS IN 1995
The USA lost to Norway 1-0 in the semifinals of the 1995 World Cup (right). Norway went on to win the World Cup, beating Germany 2-0 in the Final.

MICHELLE AKERS
Michelle Akers has scored more goals for the USA than anyone else and she was the top goalscorer in the 1991 World Cup tournament with ten goals.

Mia Hamm (right) at the Olympics

OLYMPIC CHAMPIONS
At the Atlanta Games in 1996, the competition was much stiffer than in the 1995 World Cup, but after defeating Norway in the semifinals, the USA went on to beat China and take gold.

Nigeria Football Association, founded in 1945

NIGERIA

With the emergence of Africa as a mighty force in world football, it was inevitable that before long an African nation would win a major international title. That honour fell to Nigeria when they became Olympic champions in 1996. This much deserved victory came as no surprise, because Nigeria had finished top of their first stage group in the 1994 World Cup. They had also come close to beating eventual finalists Italy in the second stage of that tournament. Nigeria have won the African Nations Cup twice, in 1980 and 1994.

Nigeria's team colours: green shirts, green shorts, and green socks

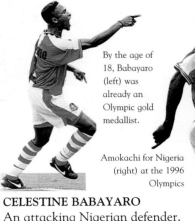

Nigeria's players celebrating their Under-17 World Championship victory in 1985

THE YOUNG PRETENDERS
Nigeria's potential was evident when they won the first ever Under-17 World Championships in 1985, beating West Germany 2-0. They won again in 1993, beating Ghana 2-1.

NWANKWO KANU
As the inspirational captain of Nigeria, Kanu was their highest goalscorer in the 1996 Olympic Games. Almost all the best Nigerian players, including Kanu, have played for European club sides.

Nwankwo Kanu was named African Footballer of the Year in 1996.

By the age of 18, Babayaro (left) was already an Olympic gold medallist.

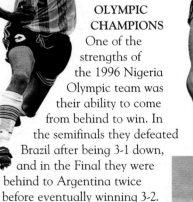

Amokachi for Nigeria (right) at the 1996 Olympics

CELESTINE BABAYARO
An attacking Nigerian defender, Babayaro was bought by Chelsea from Belgian team Anderlecht in a £2.25 million transfer deal in 1997.

OLYMPIC CHAMPIONS
One of the strengths of the 1996 Nigeria Olympic team was their ability to come from behind to win. In the semifinals they defeated Brazil after being 3-1 down, and in the Final they were behind to Argentina twice before eventually winning 3-2.

 What is the nickname of the Nigerian team?

TEAMS TO WATCH

Australia in 1997. Many Australian players currently play in Europe and the national side could soon be a World Cup contender.

ONLY SIX DIFFERENT countries have been World Cup champions since the tournament began in 1930. Between them Brazil, Italy, Germany, Argentina, Uruguay, and England have won all fifteen of the finals. However, with national teams the world over becoming stronger all the time, it surely can't be long before new names start appearing at the top of the roll of honour. Here are just a few of the countries that might reach those heady heights in years to come.

Ramon Vega and Johann Vogel for Switzerland against Paul Gascoigne for England in the opening match of the 1996 European Championship

SCANDINAVIA AND SWITZERLAND

Denmark are achieving their potential, having won the 1992 European Championship. Sweden reached the semifinals of the same tournament, losing 3-2 to the other eventual finalists, Germany. Switzerland qualified for the European Championship for the first time in 1996.

Robert Prosinecki for Croatia and Sergen Yalcin for Turkey in a match from the 1996 European Championship. Croatia won the game 1-0.

TURKEY

Another country who could achieve success soon is Turkey. At club level, their sides Galatasaray and Fenerbahce are more than holding their own in European competitions, and qualifying for the European Championship in 1996 was a great boost for the national side. To date, Turkey's only appearance in a World Cup finals tournament was in 1954.

An outstanding performance by Bulgaria (in the red and white strip) against Germany. It brought them a 2-1 victory in the quarter finals of the 1994 World Cup.

BULGARIA

After knocking out Germany in the 1994 World Cup quarter finals, Bulgaria were denied a place in the final when they were narrowly defeated by Italy in the semifinals. In Stoichkov, the joint top scorer of the 1994 tournament with six goals, they possess a world class player.

Cameroon (in the red and green strip) against South Africa in the African Nations Cup in 1996

CAMEROON

The best bet for a new name on the World Cup trophy must surely come from Africa, with Cameroon high on the list of likely winners. They qualified for the 1982, 1990, and 1994 World Cup finals, and were unlucky to lose 3-2 to England after extra time in the 1990 quarter finals.

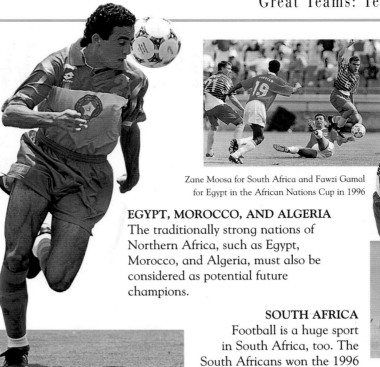

Mohammed Samadi for Morocco in a 1994 World Cup match against Holland

Zane Moosa for South Africa and Fawzi Gamal for Egypt in the African Nations Cup in 1996

EGYPT, MOROCCO, AND ALGERIA

The traditionally strong nations of Northern Africa, such as Egypt, Morocco, and Algeria, must also be considered as potential future champions.

Below, Philemon Massinga of South Africa and Bekhti Karim of Algeria in the African Nations Cup in 1996

SOUTH AFRICA

Football is a huge sport in South Africa, too. The South Africans won the 1996 African Nations Cup, beating Tunisia 2-0 in the Final.

SOUTH KOREA, JAPAN, AND CHINA

As co-hosts of the 2002 World Cup, South Korea and Japan have high hopes of glory. The South Koreans have already proved themselves in previous finals and, with Japan's J-League building a base of home-grown players, Japan may also prove to be a strong footballing nation. China is another nation with massive potential. Football is growing in popularity there, and their women's team could well bring home their first trophy.

Miura for Japan and Neville for England in the Umbro Cup in 1995

Japan's Kazuyoshi Miura scores a goal against China in the 1996 Asia Games.

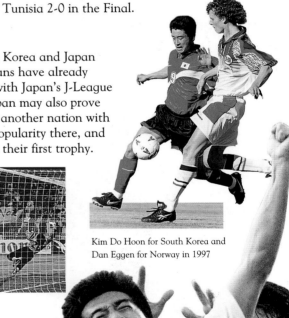

Kim Do Hoon for South Korea and Dan Eggen for Norway in 1997

Terry Venables as Australia's coach

Seo Jung Won for South Korea after scoring an equalizer in a 2-2 draw with Spain in the 1994 World Cup

AUSTRALIA

The appointment of ex-England coach Terry Venables as the coach for Australia has shown how serious Australia is about improving its status in the game. However, soccer still ranks behind cricket, rugby, and Australian Rules football in Australian sporting affections.

Pele celebrates his goal in the 1970 World Cup Final.

GREAT PLAYERS

Every once in a while a footballer comes along who

really stands out. Players such as Pele, Beckenbauer,

or Banks with their breathtaking skill and ability

earn the title of superstar.

PELE

EDSON ARANTES DO NASCIMENTO, or Pele, is the greatest player the world has ever seen. A forward, he played with incredible skill, creativity, and strength. He mesmerized defenders the world over, who, even if they could get near him, often had no way of stopping him. Over the years, many players have been heralded as the "new Pele", but none have been worthy of the title. There was, and always will be, only one Pele.

Pele with the Jules Rimet trophy, 1970

Factfile

Born:	23.10.40 Tres Coracoes, Brazil
Clubs:	**Santos** 1956-74
	1144 appearances,
	1090 goals
	New York Cosmos 1975-77
	105 appearances, 55 goals
International Record:	
	Brazil 1957-71
	92 appearances, 77 goals

TEENAGE GLORY
Aged just 17, Pele scored his first ever World Cup goal in Brazil's 1-0 victory over Wales in the 1958 tournament in Sweden. In the semifinal against France he scored a hat trick, and his two goals in the 5-2 final victory over Sweden gave Brazil the first of their World Cup triumphs.

A spectacular overhead kick from Pele during a 1965 match between Brazil and Belgium.

Pele collects the ball after scoring a penalty for Santos against Vasco da Gama on 19 November 1969. It was his 1000th goal.

GOALS, GOALS, AND MORE GOALS
Goals were Pele's trademark. His devastating pace and unsurpassed ball control made him a lethal striker. In his senior career he scored an astounding 1283 goals in total.

Pele celebrates a goal in the 1970 World Cup Final between Brazil and Italy. He scored Brazil's first goal and created two more, contributing to Brazil's 4-1 win.

OLDER, WISER, AND JUST AS BRILLIANT
At the age of 29, Pele was at the peak of his powers. He played in every round of the 1970 World Cup. His dummies, shots from the half-way line, and brilliant goals, inspired Brazil's famous World Cup victory.

A NEW CAREER
In 1975, Pele joined the New York Cosmos, helping to establish the popularity of football in the United States. He retired in 1977 after the Cosmos had won the NASL Soccer Bowl. Today Pele remains in the public eye as Brazil's Minister for Sport.

FRANZ BECKENBAUER

ON TOP OF THE WORLD AT LAST
Beckenbauer finally tasted World Cup success as captain of West Germany in their 2-1 victory over the much-fancied Dutch side in 1974.

GERMANY'S GREATEST PLAYER, Franz Beckenbauer was known as the "Kaiser". From his position as sweeper in the heart of the defence, he was able to influence and organize the whole team. His all-round ability and leadership qualities led him to World Cup glory as a player in 1974 and as manager of West Germany in 1990. As captain of Bayern Munich he won three European Cup winners' medals and was twice named European Footballer of the Year. He then had three NASL Soccer Bowl victories with the New York Cosmos.

Factfile
Born: 11.9.45 Munich, Germany
Clubs: **Bayern Munich** 1962-76
396 appearances, 44 goals
New York Cosmos 1976-83
132 appearances, 23 goals
SV Hamburg 1983-84
28 appearances, 0 goals
International Record:
West Germany 1967-74
103 appearances, 13 goals

Beckenbauer shoots for goal in the 1976 European Cup Final between Bayern Munich and Saint-Etienne.

Beckenbauer developed the role of "attacking sweeper", turning defence into attack for Bayern Munich and W. Germany.

A HAT TRICK OF VICTORIES
It was definitely Beckenbauer's year in 1974. With him in the driving seat, Bayern Munich became the first German side to win the European Cup, beating Atletico Madrid. Bayern then went on to repeat Ajax's three European Cup wins in a row by beating Leeds United in 1975 and Saint-Etienne in 1976.

MANAGING SUCCESS
When West Germany became World Cup champions in 1990, Beckenbauer became the first person to win the World Cup as both captain and manager. He later moved into club management with Bayern Munich and now has a role as club president.

Beckenbauer as W. Germany's manager in 1990

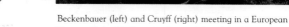

Beckenbauer (left) and Cruyff (right) meeting in a European Cup match in 1973 between Bayern Munich and Ajax.

SWEEPING UP
Playing behind the back markers, the sweeper casts a masterful eye over the proceedings, making crucial tackles, distributing the ball, and foraging forward. Franz Beckenbauer brought an attacking approach to the role and set the standard for all who followed.

JOHAN CRUYFF

JOHAN CRUYFF'S SKILFUL "TURN" in the 1974 World Cup has probably been copied by more players the world over than any other technique. A graceful, dominating figure on the pitch, his passing ability was second to none. He led Holland to the 1974 World Cup Final and, with Dutch side Ajax, he won three European Cups in a row. He went on to play for Barcelona and after helping them to a Spanish League victory, he later became their most successful manager.

Factfile

Born: 25.4.47 Amsterdam, Holland
Clubs: Ajax 1965-73 311 appearances, 252 goals; **Barcelona** 1973-78 186 appearances, 61 goals; **Los Angeles Aztecs** 1979 27 appearances, 14 goals; **Washington Diplomats** 1980-81 32 appearances, 12 goals; **Levante** 1981 10 appearances, 2 goals; **Ajax** 1981-83 46 appearances, 16 goals; **Feyenoord** 1983-84 44 appearances, 13 goals
International Record: Holland 1966-78 48 appearances, 33 goals

Cruyff was the first player to be voted European Footballer of the Year for three seasons running.

Johan Cruyff demonstrates his spectacular skills against defender, Berti Vogts, in the 1974 World Cup Final against W. Germany.

NIMBLE FEET

Cruyff became known for his astounding ball control. He would bring his foot over the ball, push it back, and then twist his body round to leave the defender totally bamboozled.

SO NEAR AND YET ...

The 1974 World Cup finals tournament gave Cruyff the chance to really shine on the world stage. His brilliance helped Holland to the Final, but they were unable to defeat the hosts, West Germany, and Cruyff had to be content with a runners-up medal after losing 2-1.

Cruyff in his role as manager of Barcelona talking to defender Albert Ferrer, 1996

THE BOSS

As manager of Barcelona, Cruyff led the Spanish side to their first ever European Cup victory in 1992. He also continued his tradition of winning things in a row as, with him at the helm, Barcelona won the championship from 1991 to 1994. He left Barcelona in 1996.

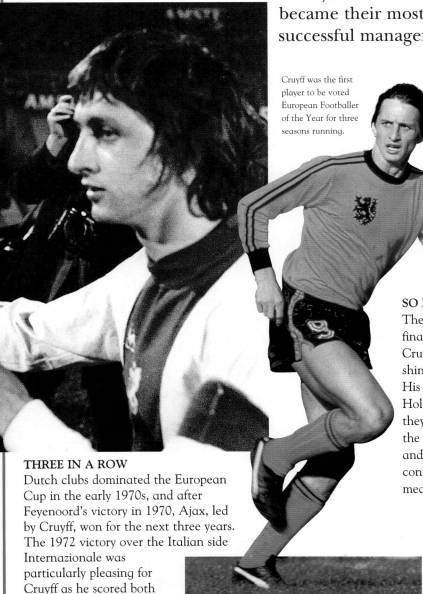

THREE IN A ROW

Dutch clubs dominated the European Cup in the early 1970s, and after Feyenoord's victory in 1970, Ajax, led by Cruyff, won for the next three years. The 1972 victory over the Italian side Internazionale was particularly pleasing for Cruyff as he scored both goals in the 2-0 win.

RUUD GULLIT

The Dutch star during the 1992 European Championship semifinal against Denmark. The final score was a 2-2 draw, but Denmark won the penalty shoot-out 5-4.

RUUD GULLIT WAS ONE of the game's most versatile players. Whether in attack, midfield, or even defence, he had a commanding presence, passing the ball with pinpoint accuracy, dribbling past defenders as if they weren't there, or powerfully heading the ball into the net. In 1988 Ruud Gullit lifted the European Championship trophy to mark his nation's finest moment.

Factfile

Born:	1.9.62 Amsterdam, Holland
Clubs:	**Haarlem** 1979-82
	89 appearances, 30 goals
	Feyenoord 1982-85
	85 appearances, 30 goals
	PSV Eindhoven 1985-87
	68 appearances, 46 goals
	AC Milan 1987-93
	117 appearances, 35 goals
	Sampdoria 1993-94
	31 appearances, 15 goals
	AC Milan 1994
	8 appearances, 3 goals
	Sampdoria 1994-95
	22 appearances, 9 goals
	Chelsea 1995-
	31 appearances, 3 goals
International Record:	
	Holland 1981-93
	65 appearances, 16 goals

Ruud Gullit as captain of Holland in the 1988 European Championship Final. Holland beat the USSR 2-0.

Knee injuries badly affected Gullit's career at the beginning of the 1990s, but he injected a new lease of life into his game with a move to Chelsea in 1995.

THE MAGIC OF MILAN
In his time at AC Milan, Gullit won three Italian League championships and two European Cups. He was voted European and World Footballer of the Year in his first season with the club, and dedicated both awards to Nelson Mandela, who was still imprisoned in South Africa at the time.

A NEW CHALLENGE
In 1995 Gullit joined top English club Chelsea, and in 1996 he took over as player-manager. In his first season as manager, Gullit led Chelsea to the 1997 English FA Cup Final, which they won against Middlesbrough 2-0.

Ruud Gullit playing for AC Milan against Napoli, 1989

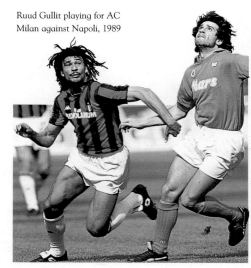

DIEGO MARADONA

The powerful Maradona could find a way through the strongest defence.

UNDOUBTEDLY THE BEST player of his generation, when Diego Maradona was playing at the peak of his game, he was unstoppable. Small and powerful, his control was immaculate and he could weave his way past defenders effortlessly. He captained Argentina to World Cup victory in 1986, and in 1987 and 1990 helped Italian side Napoli win the Italian League championship. He also led Argentina to the 1990 World Cup Final, which they lost to West Germany.

Factfile

Born: 30.10.60 Buenos Aires, Argentina
Clubs: **Argentinos Juniors** 1976-80
116 appearances, 28 goals
Boca Juniors 1980-82
40 appearances, 28 goals
Barcelona 1982-84
36 appearances, 22 goals
Napoli 1984-91
186 appearances, 81 goals
Seville 1992-93
26 appearances, 5 goals
Newells Old Boys 1993-94
13 appearances, 4 goals
Boca Juniors 1995
24 appearances, 8 goals
International Record:
Argentina 1977-94
90 appearances, 33 goals

The 1986 World Cup saw Maradona playing the finest football of his career. His amazingly accurate pass in the Final led to Jorge Burruchaga scoring the winner in Argentina's 3-2 victory against W. Germany.

A HELPING HAND
Maradona scored both goals in Argentina's 2-1 World Cup quarter final win against England in 1986. His first was regarded by many as a hand ball. The second was one of the greatest solo efforts in World Cup history.

NEAPOLITAN HEAVEN
When Maradona was transferred from Barcelona to Napoli for £5 million in 1984, the Italian club were expecting a big return for their money. They were not disappointed as he led them to an Italian League and Cup double in 1987, and their first ever European trophy when Napoli won the UEFA Cup in 1989.

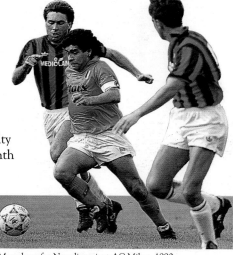

THE BOTTOM OF THE WORLD
In 1991 Maradona was found guilty of drug abuse and given a 15-month worldwide ban. On his return, he still looked formidable, but was thrown out of the 1994 World Cup when he failed a drugs test again. In 1995 Maradona returned to the game, playing with Boca Juniors in Argentina.

Maradona for Napoli against AC Milan, 1990

GEORGE BEST

A YEAR TO REMEMBER
In 1968 Best scored Manchester United's second goal as they defeated Benfica of Portugal 4-1 to become the first English club to win the European Cup. That year he was also named European Footballer of the Year.

BEING DESCRIBED BY PELE AS, "the best footballer I have ever seen", is about as high an accolade as any footballer could wish for. George Best was British football's most naturally gifted player, who was able to conjure up goals from the most unlikely of positions. He moved with grace and athleticism, and his magical ball skills and marvellous balance left defenders quaking in his wake. The lad from Northern Ireland became Britain's first "superstar" footballer.

Factfile

Born:	22.5.46 Belfast, N. Ireland
Clubs:	**Manchester United** 1963-75
	361 appearances, 137 goals
	Stockport County 1975-76
	3 appearances, 2 goals
	Los Angeles Aztecs 1976-78
	61 appearances, 29 goals
	Cork Celtic 1976
	16 appearances, 4 goals
	Fulham 1976-78
	42 appearances, 8 goals
	Fort Lauderdale Strikers 1978-79
	33 appearances, 7 goals
	Hibernian 1979-80
	27 appearances, 4 goals
	San Jose Earthquakes 1980-83
	56 appearances, 21 goals
	Bournemouth 1983-84
	5 appearances, 0 goals

International Record: N. Ireland 1964-78 37 appearances, 9 goals

LIFE IN THE FAST LANE
Best led a flamboyant lifestyle, and was often seen in casinos and nightclubs. It was believed that this had an effect on his game and many feel he never truly fulfilled his potential.

George Best for N. Ireland against Peter Storey for England

SIXTH HEAVEN
On 7 February 1970, Manchester United beat Northampton Town 8-2 in an FA Cup fifth round game. Best scored six goals that day, a club record that still stands today.

THE HOLY TRINITY
Best was at his peak during the latter half of the 1960s. Together with Bobby Charlton and Denis Law up front, Best formed a strike force that propelled Manchester United to the English League title in 1965 and 1967.

Best was one of the deadliest finishers in the English League. He could also tackle as effectively as any defender and his superb dribbling skills made him a delight to watch.

MICHEL PLATINI

THE GREATEST PERIOD in French footballing history is without doubt the mid-1980s. With Michel Platini as captain, France won the European Championship in 1984, playing football that was both exhilarating and flowing. Platini was the general, leading a team packed with talent from midfield. He could pass the ball with pinpoint accuracy from one end of the pitch to the other and was deadly with free kicks just outside the opposition's penalty area.

Factfile

Born: 21.6.55 Joeuf, France
Clubs: **Nancy Lorraine** 1972-79
175 appearances, 98 goals
St-Etienne 1979-82
107 appearances, 58 goals
Juventus 1982-87
147 appearances, 68 goals
International Record:
France 1976-87
72 appearances, 41 goals

Completing a hat trick against Belgium in 1984

THE AGONY …

After battling to a 3-3 draw against West Germany in the 1982 World Cup semifinal, France and Platini suffered the pain of being the first team to go out of a World Cup in a penalty shoot-out. The Germans won the shoot-out 5-4.

Platini, the French Captain, holds the European Championship trophy.

… AND THE ECSTASY

It was a different story for Platini in 1984. With the European Championship held on their own soil, France dominated the tournament, playing some brilliant football. Platini was outstanding, and was on the score-sheet in every game, including the Final against Spain, in which he scored the opening goal.

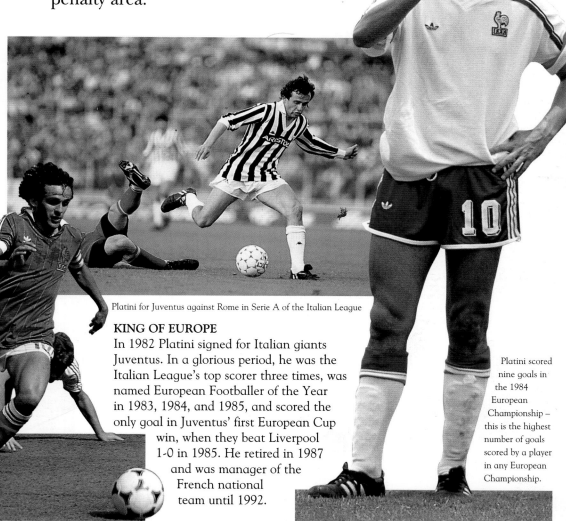

Platini for Juventus against Rome in Serie A of the Italian League

KING OF EUROPE

In 1982 Platini signed for Italian giants Juventus. In a glorious period, he was the Italian League's top scorer three times, was named European Footballer of the Year in 1983, 1984, and 1985, and scored the only goal in Juventus' first European Cup win, when they beat Liverpool 1-0 in 1985. He retired in 1987 and was manager of the French national team until 1992.

Platini scored nine goals in the 1984 European Championship – this is the highest number of goals scored by a player in any European Championship.

BOBBY CHARLTON

Bobby Charlton still holds the record for the highest number of goals scored for England.

SIR BOBBY CHARLTON is England's most famous footballer. He was a World Cup winner in 1966 and, with Manchester United, he won three English League championships and a European Cup winners' medal. A midfielder with a ferocious shot, he scored two goals in Manchester United's 4-1 win over Benfica in the 1968 European Cup Final.

Factfile

Born:	11.10.37 Ashington, England
Clubs:	**Manchester United 1954-73**
	754 appearances, 247 goals
	Preston North End 1974-75
	38 appearances, 8 goals
International Record:	
	England 1958-70
	106 appearances, 49 goals

WHAT A SHOT!
Charlton had a powerful shot due to his impeccable sense of timing. His best goals – many of which thundered into the net from way outside the penalty area – are among the most spectacular ever seen in the English League.

EUSEBIO

ONE OF MANY players dubbed "the new Pele", Eusebio da Silva Ferreira probably came nearer than most to deserving it. He was a fast, skilful attacker at the heart of the Benfica side of the early 1960s. He was the top scorer in the 1966 World Cup with nine goals, and has scored more international goals than any other Portuguese player.

Factfile

Born:	25.1.42 Lourenço Marques, Mozambique
Club:	**Benfica 1961-74**
	365 appearances, 383 goals
International Record:	
	Portugal 1961-73
	64 appearances, 41 goals

Eusebio pictured in 1973, wearing Benfica's team colours

PLAYING FOR BENFICA
In the late 1950s and early 1960s, Real Madrid were the side to beat. When they came up against Benfica and Eusebio in the 1962 European Cup Final, they were finally to meet their match. In an outstanding game, two goals from Eusebio helped his side to come out on top with a score of 5-3.

FERENC PUSKAS

FERENC PUSKAS LED HUNGARY during their greatest period. Known as the "Galloping Major", due to his rank in the army, Puskas possessed a lethal left foot and tantalized defenders with his great skill and close ball control. He led Hungary to Olympic victory in 1952 and the World Cup Final in 1954, which they lost 3-2 to West Germany. His greatest success at club level came in Spain with Real Madrid, with whom he won the European Cup in 1960. He was top scorer in the Spanish League four times.

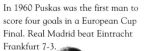

Factfile

Born:	2.4.27 Budapest, Hungary
Clubs:	**Kispet**
	(later named Honved)
	1943-55 290 appearances,
	319 goals
	Real Madrid 1958-66
	261 appearances, 232 goals
International Record:	
	Hungary 1945-56
	84 appearances, 82 goals
	Spain 1962
	4 appearances, 0 goals

In 1960 Puskas was the first man to score four goals in a European Cup Final. Real Madrid beat Eintracht Frankfurt 7-3.

Puskas exchanges flags with the England captain in 1953.

ONE IN THE EYE FOR ENGLAND
When Hungary played England in 1953, England had never lost at Wembley to foreign opposition. But Hungary shattered that record, beating England 6-3. Puskas scored two that day, one of which is notable for the way he dragged the ball back with the sole of his foot before swivelling and firing a left-foot shot past the England goalkeeper.

ALFREDO DI STEFANO

REAL MADRID DOMINATED European football in the late 1950s and early 1960s. That superiority was in no small part thanks to Alfredo Di Stefano. His clever reading of the game and immaculate sense of when to release the ball made him a force to be reckoned with. Internationally, he played for Argentina and Spain. He was once kidnapped for three days while playing for Real Madrid in Venezuela.

Factfile

Born:	4.7.26 Buenos Aires, Argentina
Clubs:	**Huracan** 1944-45
	45 appearances, 29 goals; **River Plate** 1946-49 66 appearances,
	50 goals; **Millionarios** 1949-53
	290 appearances, 260 goals;
	Real Madrid 1953-64
	624 appearances, 405 goals;
	Español 1964-65
	16 appearances, 4 goals
International Record:	
	Argentina 1947-48
	8 appearances, 5 goals
	Spain 1957-61
	31 appearances, 21 goals

FIVE GREAT FINALS
Real Madrid won the first five European Cups between 1956 and 1960. Di Stefano scored in every Final, including a hat trick in their legendary 7-3 victory over Eintracht Frankfurt in 1960.

Di Stefano equalizes for Real Madrid in the 1960 European Cup Final against Eintracht Frankfurt at Hampden Park, Glasgow.

KENNY DALGLISH

PROBABLY THE GREATEST Scottish player ever, Dalglish had incredible skill and determination and could turn defenders inside out. His achievements as a player and a manager are unmatched in British football. He became player-manager of Liverpool in 1985 and managed Blackburn Rovers to the English League championship in 1995. He is now managing Newcastle United.

Factfile

Born: 4.3.51 Glasgow, Scotland
Clubs: **Celtic** 1967-77
204 appearances, 112 goals
Liverpool 1977-90
354 appearances, 118 goals
International Record:
Scotland 1972-87
102 appearances, 30 goals

Dalglish for Liverpool with Trevor Peake of Coventry

A WEE SCOTTISH LAD

Dalglish made his debut for Celtic at the age of 17. By the time he left to go to Liverpool in 1977, he had won four Scottish League and four Scottish Cup winners' medals. His hallmarks were excellent close ball control and an ability to shield the ball from defenders. He also had a keen eye for a defence-splitting pass.

ROGER MILLA

THE FIRST MAN to be named African Footballer of the Year twice, first in 1976 and then again in 1990, Cameroon's Roger Milla really came to the attention of the world's footballing elite during the 1990 World Cup. Cameroon's progression to the quarter finals put African football on the map. In Roger Milla they had a hugely talented showman, who liked nothing more than to entertain the crowds with his great skill and goalscoring abilities.

Factfile

Born: 20.5.52 Cameroon
Clubs: **Leopard Douala** 1968-73
Tonnerre Yaounde 1973-77
Valenciennes 1977-79
Monaco 1979-80
Bastia 1980-84
St-Etienne 1984-86
Montpellier 1986-88
Toulouse 1988-89
St-Pierroise 1989
(Retired 1989-90)
Puebla 1991
International Record:
Cameroon 1972-94
Complete records for goals and appearances not available.

Milla is both the oldest player to appear and the oldest to score a goal in a World Cup finals tournament. The latter came against Russia in the 1994 World Cup. He was then 42 years of age.

GOAL CELEBRATION

Roger Milla can lay claim to having started the trend of unusual goal celebrations. After each of his four goals in the 1990 World Cup he ran to the corner flag and wiggled round it.

KARL-HEINZ RUMMENIGGE

ARGUABLY WEST GERMANY'S most important player in the late 1970s and early 1980s, Rummenigge was hugely influential during his country's World Cup campaigns of 1978, 1982, and 1986. Named European Footballer of the Year twice, he has won European Cup and World Club Championship winners' medals.

Factfile

Born:	25.9.55 Lippstadt, W. Germany
Clubs:	**Bayern Munich** 1974-84 300 appearances, 162 goals **Internazionale** 1984-87 64 appearances, 24 goals **Servette** 1987-89 50 appearances, 34 goals
International Record:	**West Germany** 1976-86 95 appearances, 45 goals

OUTSTANDING SCORER

Rummenigge scored five goals in the 1982 World Cup and was on the score-sheet when West Germany were beaten 3-2 by Argentina in the Final of the 1986 tournament.

Rummenigge leaves another defender flailing in his wake.

TWO GREAT VICTORIES

In 1976 Rummenigge was on the Bayern Munich side that defeated Saint-Etienne 1-0 to win the European Cup. Later that year, he helped the club to a 2-0 victory on aggregate over two legs against Brazilian team Cruzeiro, to win the World Club Cup.

LEV YASHIN

INVARIABLY CLAD ALL IN BLACK, the Russian goalkeeper Lev Yashin had a dogged determination and competitive spirit that was second to none. Coupled with incredible reflexes and agility, he possessed great anticipation and was a brilliant shot-stopper. He was his country's goalkeeper for twenty years and, with his club Dynamo Moscow, he won four Soviet League championships.

Factfile

Born:	22.10.29 Moscow, Russia
Club:	**Dynamo Moscow** 1951-70 326 appearances
International Record:	**Soviet Union** 1954-70 78 appearances

UNIQUE AWARDS

In 1963 Yashin was named European Footballer of the Year and he remains to this day the only goalkeeper to have been given that honour. He is also the only footballer to have been awarded the Soviet Union's Order of Lenin, which he received in 1969.

AN EXCEPTIONAL PERFORMANCE

Yashin played superbly throughout the first European Championship tournament in 1960, and was in excellent form during the 2-1 final victory against Yugoslavia.

Another dynamic save by Yashin (left), limiting the Soviet defeat at the hands of W. Germany in the 1966 World Cup semifinals. The final score was 2-1.

Punching away a corner in the 1958 World Cup during a 2-2 draw with England

GORDON BANKS

BANKS WAS HAILED as the greatest keeper in the world between 1966 and 1970. His amazing athleticism allowed him to pull off saves that others would have no hope of reaching. As the last line of defence, he was inspirational. Sadly, he had to quit in 1972 after losing an eye in a car accident.

Banks saves the ball (left) in the 1966 World Cup Final against W. Germany, which England won 4-2.

Banks makes his famous save, clearing Pele's header in the 1970 World Cup.

THE WORLD'S GREATEST SAVE
When Pele headed Jairzinho's cross towards the net during the 1970 World Cup clash between England and Brazil, it looked a certain goal. Banks raced across and dived, but appeared to be beaten by the ball's bounce. Incredibly, he managed to twist upwards in mid-air and deflect the ball over the crossbar.

DINO ZOFF

Zoff leaps to make a save, securing Italy's 3-1 victory over W. Germany in the 1982 World Cup Final.

ITALIAN DEFENCES HAVE always been notoriously hard to break down, but when Dino Zoff was in goal, that task was made much harder. A tall, commanding figure, he had a steely resolve that made him almost impossible to beat. His proudest moment was captaining Italy to World Cup triumph in 1982. As a player with club side Juventus, he won six Italian League titles and the UEFA Cup.

A CLEAN SHEET
Between September 1973 and June 1974, Zoff did not concede a goal at international level for an incredible 1143 minutes. The run extended over twelve matches and was only broken when Haiti scored against Italy in the World Cup.

Zoff was the first Italian to make 100 international appearances.

The winning goal from the 1986 World Cup Final

THE FIFA WORLD CUP

It is the dream of every footballer to win the World Cup.

Those who have done so can rightly call themselves the best in the

world. Held every four years, the World Cup has been a showcase

for some of the greatest football ever seen, played by some

of the greatest players ever known.

A DREAM BEGINS

French sculptor, Albert Lafleur, designed the World Cup trophy, which became known as the Jules Rimet trophy.

IN THE EARLY 1900S the amateur Olympic football tournament was considered by many to be the world's premier international football competition. However, as teams became increasingly professional, there was a need for a new tournament. In 1928 Jules Rimet, the then president of FIFA and the French Football Association, put forward a motion that there should be a World Cup competition open to every nation and held every four years. The motion was passed and the following year Uruguay, whose team were Olympic champions, hosted the first World Cup.

Jules Rimet presents the World Cup trophy to the President of the Uruguayan Football Association at the start of the first tournament.

1930 URUGUAY

Argentina's goalkeeper, Botasso, is unable to stop Dorado's shot. It was Uruguay's first goal in the Final.

ALTHOUGH THE host nation offered to pay everyone's travel expenses, only four European teams, France, Belgium, Yugoslavia, and Romania, made the long boat trip to Uruguay. They were joined by eight teams from South and Central America, plus the USA, and on 13 July 1930 the first World Cup competition kicked off with France against Mexico (France won 4-1).

THE FINALISTS

Argentina	Paraguay
Belgium	Peru
Bolivia	Romania
Brazil	Uruguay
Chile	USA
France	Yugoslavia
Mexico	

THE TOURNAMENT
The 13 teams were split into four groups and the winners of each group progressed to the semifinals. Both semifinals ended with 6-1 scores. Argentina beat the USA, and Uruguay beat Yugoslavia.

Uruguay in action

THE FINAL:
Uruguay 4 Argentina 2
With Uruguay as Olympic champions and Argentina as South American champions, there couldn't have been two more apt opponents for the first World Cup Final. The match was very much a game of two halves. Uruguay scored in the 12th minute, but Argentina equalized and then scored again to lead at half-time. The second half, however, belonged to Uruguay. They scored three times to win 4-2 and become the first world champions.

Argentina's Pecucelle scores to equalize in the Final, but Uruguay went on to win 4-2.

1934 ITALY

THE SECOND WORLD CUP was the first in which teams went through a qualifying tournament. Out of the 31 teams entering the qualifying stage, 16 got through to the finals tournament, which kicked off on 27 May. Holders Uruguay did not enter.

THE FINALISTS
Argentina	Hungary
Austria	Italy
Belgium	Romania
Brazil	Spain
Czech.	Sweden
Egypt	Switzerland
France	USA
Germany	
Holland	

Italy's Allemandi against the USA keeper

Schiavio's spectacular volley for Italy, watched by team mates Meazza and Orsi

THE TOURNAMENT
In the finals tournament the 16 teams were drawn against each other in a straightforward knockout competition. Italy, who had cruised past the USA 7-1 in the first stage, needed a replay to beat Spain 1-0 in the next, and then beat Austria 1-0 to reach the Final. Czechoslovakia beat Germany 3-1 in the other semifinal.

THE FINAL:
Italy 2 Czechoslovakia 1
(After extra time)
In front of 55,000 people, it was the Czechs who scored first in the 70th minute. They could have sealed victory, but missed two good chances. Then, with the crowd desperate for a home victory, Italy equalized in the 82nd minute. In extra time it was the Italians who managed to summon up more energy and, when Schiavio scored after 95 minutes, they held on to win.

Manager Vittorio Pozzo carried by his victorious team

1938 FRANCE

FRANCE WAS CHOSEN to host the 1938 World Cup ahead of Argentina, a decision which meant that this tournament became the least representative ever. Only three non-European teams were involved and two of those, Cuba and the Dutch East Indies, were there because of byes in the qualifying stages.

Italy celebrate after becoming world champions for the second time.

THE FINAL:
Italy 4 Hungary 2
Hungary had high hopes of defeating World Cup holders Italy, but Italy's speed and goalscoring ability saw them race to a 3-1 lead by half-time. Sarosi scored for Hungary in the 70th minute, but 12 minutes later, Italy's star Piola made it 4-2 to give Italy the second win they had hoped for.

THE FINALISTS
Belgium	Hungary
Brazil	Italy
Cuba	Norway
Czech.	Poland
Dutch E. Indies	Romania
France	Sweden
Germany	Switzerland
Holland	

Peracio heads Brazil's fourth goal past Poland's goalkeeper Madejski.

THE TOURNAMENT
The 1934 format was retained. The outstanding match of the first stage saw Brazil defeat Poland 6-5, whilst Cuba provided the shock by beating Romania 2-1. In the semifinals Hungary beat Sweden 5-1 and Italy beat Brazil 2-1.

The winning Italian team

 Top goalscorers 1934: Nejedly 4 (Czechoslovakia); Schiavio 4 (Italy); Conen 4 (Germany).
1938: Leonidas 8 (Brazil); Szengeller 7 (Hungary); Piola 5 (Italy).

71

1950 BRAZIL

THE SECOND WORLD WAR put a stop to the World Cup for 12 years, but in South America football was barely affected so Brazil was chosen to host the 1950 tournament. Again, the qualifying competition was a little disorganized and a number of teams dropped out. Among the final 13, England made a first appearance, and Uruguay returned for the first time since winning in 1930.

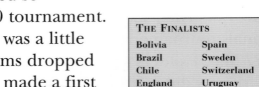

The opening ceremony was a lavish affair at the newly-built Maracana Stadium.

Above, Obdulio Varela, captain of the Uruguay team.

Below, the USA defeated England 1-0 in this first stage match.

THE FINALISTS	
Bolivia	Spain
Brazil	Sweden
Chile	Switzerland
England	Uruguay
Italy	USA
Mexico	Yugoslavia
Paraguay	

Brazil against Mexico in a first stage match that they won 4-0. Playing in front of home crowds, Brazil had high hopes of reaching the Final.

THE FIRST STAGE GROUPS

The teams were split into four groups. Group Four consisted of only Uruguay and Bolivia due to the last-minute withdrawal of France after they decided that they didn't want to make the journey to Brazil. England's debut was notable only because they suffered one of the most surprising upsets in international football by losing 1-0 to the USA in the first stage.

THE ROUTE TO THE FINAL

The four group winners, Brazil, Uruguay, Sweden, and Spain, went into a final group where each team played each other. Brazil beat Sweden and Spain, 7-1 and 6-1 respectively. Uruguay defeated Sweden and drew with Spain, so the last group match between the two South American giants was to be decisive.

THE FINAL:
Uruguay 2 Brazil 1

Due to the final stage being a group competition, Brazil only needed a draw against Uruguay to win the tournament. On 16 July a crowd made up almost entirely of Brazilians was not even considering anything less. When Friaca scored for Brazil two minutes into the second half, everything seemed to be going to plan. Then, after 66 minutes, Uruguay's Schiaffino equalized. Incredibly, 11 minutes from the final whistle another goal, this time from Ghiggia, put Uruguay in the lead. They held on until the end of the match to become champions and thousands of Brazilians went home very disappointed.

Amid a goalmouth scramble, the referee signals the end of the Final.

1954 SWITZERLAND

IN 1946 FIFA HAD DECIDED that Switzerland should host the 1954 tournament. Switzerland was the only European contender at the time and as 1954 was also the 50th anniversary of FIFA, whose headquarters are in Zurich, Switzerland was the ideal choice. The qualifying tournament was more representative than it had been four years before, and Scotland, South Korea, and Turkey got through to the finals tournament for the first time.

Kocsis of Hungary was the top goalscorer of the 1954 finals tournament. He scored four of Hungary's eight goals against W. Germany in the first stage and 11 in the tournament as a whole.

Jules Rimet, president of FIFA, at the 1954 Final

THE FINALISTS	
Austria	Mexico
Belgium	Scotland
Brazil	S. Korea
Czech.	Switzerland
England	Turkey
France	Uruguay
Hungary	W. Germany
Italy	Yugoslavia

Hungary defeated Brazil 4-2 in this quarter final, which ended in a riot. Swiss police rushed on to the pitch to separate the fighting players. The match became known as the "Battle of Berne". Here, Humberto of Brazil is held back as police lead off Brazil's assistant coach.

THE FORMAT
The 16 teams were split into four groups. Rather oddly though, each group had two seeded teams who only played two games against the unseeded teams. The top two of each group went on to a knockout phase.

Kocsis (right) helps Hungary defeat Brazil 4-2.

THE ROUTE TO THE FINAL
Hungary were strong favourites and after thrashing South Korea 9-0 and West Germany 8-3 they seemed unstoppable. They advanced to the Final by defeating Brazil and Uruguay. There they met West Germany for the second time in the tournament. West Germany had beaten Yugoslavia and Austria in the knockout phase.

THE FINAL:
West Germany 3 Hungary 2
After their 8-3 victory over West Germany earlier in the competition, the Hungarians were confident and two goals in the first eight minutes seemed to put them on the right course. However, the Germans hit back with two goals of their own in the next eight minutes, making the score 2-2 with under a quarter of the match played. For the next 65 minutes, with the rain lashing down, Hungary besieged the German goal, but amazingly, they failed to score.

Morlock breaks through Hungary's defence to score W. Germany's first goal in the Final.

LAST MINUTES
Extra time seemed inevitable until, five minutes from the end, West Germany scored to seal victory.

 Top goalscorers: Kocsis 11 (Hungary); Morlock 8 (West Germany); Probst 6 (Austria).

1958 SWEDEN

Above, Lev Yashin for the Soviet Union fails to stop Derek Kevan's shot from crossing the line. It was the first goal for England in this match. The game ended 2-2.

THE COMPETITION STAYED in Europe in 1958, rather than returning to South America, and was the most representative yet, even though less than half of FIFA's membership entered. Argentina made a welcome return to the tournament and all four of the United Kingdom's countries qualified. Italy and Uruguay, who between them had won four of the first five championships, were both absent having failed to qualify.

Brazil beating the Soviet Union 2-0 in the first stage

THE FINALISTS

Argentina	N. Ireland
Austria	Paraguay
Brazil	Scotland
Czech.	Soviet Union
England	Sweden
France	W. Germany
Hungary	Wales
Mexico	Yugoslavia

Vava scores Brazil's fourth goal against France in their semifinal.

THE TOURNAMENT

The 16 finalists were split into four groups and this time all the teams played each other. The top two of each group progressed to a knockout phase. Sweden topped their group and defeated the Soviet Union and West Germany to get to the Final. The other side to win through were Brazil, who beat France 5-2 in their semifinal.

THE FINAL:
Brazil 5 Sweden 2

A heavily rain-sodden pitch was expected to favour home team Sweden and when they took the lead after only four minutes, Brazil might have collapsed. However, thanks to two goals by Vava, at half-time Brazil were leading 2-1. The second half belonged to the young Pele. In a dazzling display, he scored Brazil's third goal and then Zagalo made it 4-1. Sweden did pull a goal back, but Pele scored again in the 89th minute. It was the first time a team had won the World Cup outside of their own continent and the first time the world had witnessed the brilliance of Pele.

A 17-year-old Pele sheds tears of joy with Djalma Santos, Didi, and Gilmar after Brazil's win in the Final.

Above, Pele heads the ball and below, he shoots against Sweden's goalkeeper, Kalle Svensson.

1962 CHILE

CHILE WAS CHOSEN to host the 1962 World Cup largely due to the efforts of the president of the Chilean FA, Carlos Dittborn. After a massive earthquake in 1960, he summed up Chile's desperation to hold the tournament when he said, "We have nothing. That is why we must have the World Cup." Sadly, Dittborn died a month before the finals tournament. Once again, the qualifying teams were entirely from Europe and South and Central America as the teams from Africa and Asia were defeated in the qualifying stages.

Home team Chile were defeated 4-2 by Brazil in the semifinals shown above (Chile in red strip).

Uwe Seeler for W. Germany challenges Yugoslavia's goalkeeper in a quarter final match. W. Germany lost the game 1-0.

THE TOURNAMENT

The format of the competition remained the same as in 1958. Brazil and Czechoslovakia both qualified from the same group and got through to the semifinals. Brazil beat Chile 4-2 and Czechoslovakia beat Yugoslavia 3-1. Pele's tournament finished early when he was injured in the first stage.

THE FINALISTS	
Argentina	Italy
Brazil	Mexico
Bulgaria	Soviet Union
Chile	Spain
Colombia	Switzerland
Czech.	Uruguay
England	W. Germany
Hungary	Yugoslavia

Zito scores Brazil's second goal from a header in the 69th minute.

Mauro holds the Jules Rimet trophy aloft for Brazil after they retain their title as world champions.

Czech goalkeeper Schroiff fails to stop Brazil's free kick in the Final.

THE FINAL:

Brazil 3 Czechoslovakia 1
Czechoslovakia were a side with a strong defence, but little attacking flair. Yet they surprised everyone by taking the lead after 16 minutes. It was short lived however, as two minutes later Brazil equalized after a mistake by the Czech goalkeeper, Schroiff. Half-way through the second half, Brazil took the lead through Amarildo, Pele's replacement. Then another goalkeeping error allowed them to score again to win 3-1. Even without Pele, Brazil had retained their title.

1966 ENGLAND

Eusebio in tears after England defeated Portugal 2-1 in the semifinals

World Cup Willie, the official 1966 mascot

ENGLAND, SPAIN, AND WEST GERMANY all put forward bids to stage the World Cup in 1966, but in the end England was awarded the tournament. Football had come home to the country that invented the game as we know it today. The number of countries entering the qualifying stages continued to grow, with 71 teams this time. However, Africa and Asia were awarded only one place in the finals between them, so most of the teams from those continents dropped out. The eventual qualifiers for that place were North Korea.

THE FINALISTS

Argentina	Mexico
Brazil	N. Korea
Bulgaria	Portugal
Chile	Soviet Union
England	Spain
France	Switzerland
Hungary	Uruguay
Italy	W. Germany

Italy's players make a brave attempt to equalize, but North Korea were to win this first stage match 1-0 and qualify for the knockout phase.

The Soviets losing 2-1 to W. Germany in the semifinals

THE ROUTE TO THE FINAL

After topping their group, England then defeated Argentina and Portugal en route to the Final. There they met West Germany who had beaten Uruguay and the Soviet Union in the knockout phase. The North Koreans didn't quite make it to the Final after throwing away a three goal lead in their quarter final match against Portugal.

England's great defender and captain, Bobby Moore

THE FIRST STAGE

The previous format was repeated. North Korea were surprise victors over Italy and qualified for the knockout phase. Pele once again suffered injury and Brazil finished only third in their group.

THE FINAL:

England 4 West Germany 2 (After extra time)
In an even contest, Haller scored for West Germany after 13 minutes, but Hurst equalized for England by half-time. After 77 minutes Peters scored and England looked set for victory until, seconds from the end, West Germany equalized through Weber to take the game into extra time. Hurst then hit a shot against the crossbar that bounced down and out of the goal. The referee awarded a goal, much to the disgust of West Germany. However, in the dying seconds, Hurst scored again, making him the only player to score a hat trick in a World Cup Final, and ensuring England became world champions.

Top goalscorers: Eusebio 9 (Portugal); Haller 5 (West Germany); Beckenbauer 4 (West Germany).

1970 MEXICO

THE CHOICE OF MEXICO as host for the 1970 World Cup finals tournament was felt by many to be a little surprising. With the intense heat and altitude, it was thought that the quality of football might suffer. As it turned out, football blossomed. Holders England were strongly fancied to retain their title, but West Germany were to make up for their defeat in 1966. They knocked out England 3-2 in the quarter finals after extra time. Israel and El Salvador qualified for the first time, as did Morocco, who became the first African nation to compete in a finals tournament.

W. Germany's Müller brings the score to 2-1 in their semifinal against Italy. Italy went on to win 4-3.

Making one of the greatest saves of all time, Gordon Banks stops Pele's shot in this first stage match between Brazil and England. Brazil went on to beat England 1-0 with a goal from Jairzinho.

Peru beating Morocco 3-0 in the first stage

THE TOURNAMENT

The four-group format was retained. Brazil, with a fully fit Pele, won all three of their group games as did West Germany. Italy won their group despite scoring only one goal, but they improved in the quarter finals beating Mexico 4-1. Italy then secured a place in the Final after an exhilarating 4-3 semifinal win against West Germany. There they met Brazil who looked unstoppable after victories over Peru and Uruguay.

THE FINALISTS

Belgium	Mexico
Brazil	Morocco
Bulgaria	Peru
Czech.	Romania
El Salvador	Soviet Union
England	Sweden
Israel	Uruguay
Italy	W. Germany

Brazil's right-winger Jairzinho (right) scored in every game for Brazil in the 1970 finals tournament.

THE FINAL:

Brazil 4 Italy 1

In what was probably football's greatest team performance, Brazil were far too strong for Italy. Pele scored their first goal after 17 minutes. A defensive error allowed Italy to equalize with a goal from Boninsenga, but three brilliant second-half goals, the last of which was one of the most memorable goals ever, saw Brazil cruise to victory. As world champions for a third time, they were allowed to keep the Jules Rimet trophy.

Brazil's defender Brito clears Italy's cross in the Final.

Pele holding the Jules Rimet trophy

 Top goalscorers: Müller 9 (West Germany); **Jairzinho 7 (Brazil); Pele 4 (Brazil).**

1974 WEST GERMANY

WEST GERMANY WAS in a good position to take on the World Cup in 1974, having hosted the Olympic Games two years previously. Terrorism had ruined the Olympics, so security for the World Cup was particularly tight. The number of Asian and African teams entering the qualifying stages rose dramatically, although they were still fighting for only two places in the finals tournament. England failed to qualify this time, having been eliminated by Poland.

The dominating Franz Beckenbauer playing in a second stage group match against Poland that W. Germany won 1-0

The new FIFA trophy was presented for the first time in 1974.

Yugoslavia holding Brazil to a 0-0 draw in the opening match

Scotland against Yugoslavia in a first stage group match that ended as a 1-1 draw

THE TOURNAMENT

The 16 teams were still split into four groups, but this time the eight qualifiers were split into two further groups and the top team of each went on to the Final. Holland were impressive and reached their first Final. There they met the home side, West Germany.

THE FINALISTS	
Argentina	Italy
Australia	Poland
Brazil	Scotland
Bulgaria	Sweden
Chile	Uruguay
E. Germany	W. Germany
Haiti	Yugoslavia
Holland	Zaire

Müller for W. Germany scoring the winning goal in the Final against Holland.

THE FINAL:

West Germany 2 Holland 1

In an amazing start, Cruyff burst into the German penalty area and was brought down with less than a minute played. Neeskens then scored the first penalty in a World Cup Final and Holland were leading 1-0 without a German player having touched the ball! West Germany levelled the score after 25 minutes when they, too, were awarded a penalty, scored by Paul Breitner. Just before half-time, they took the lead through the irrepressible Gerd Müller. Try as they might, the Dutch couldn't break down the German defence in the second half and so the new World Cup trophy went to the host nation.

The brilliant Johan Cruyff (left) at the helm of the Holland side who played their unique brand of "total football"

The victorious team of 1974, W. Germany. Franz Beckenbauer (captain) and Helmut Schoen (coach) hold the trophy.

1978 ARGENTINA

The River Plate Stadium during the opening ceremony

ARGENTINA FINALLY STAGED a World Cup in 1978. At the time there were fears that political problems and delays in the construction of some stadiums would threaten the running of the tournament, but in the event there were no such problems. Once again, England failed to qualify, as did Uruguay, but Brazil maintained their record of playing in every finals tournament. There were still only two places in the finals for African and Asian nations, but, with more countries from these two continents entering the qualifying stages than ever before, this was the last time there would be so few.

Poland beating Tunisia 1-0 in a first stage match. Poland went on to win their first stage group. Tunisia came third, but were impressive beating Mexico 3-1 and drawing 0-0 with W. Germany.

Argentina winning 6-0 against Peru to put themselves one game away from glory

THE TOURNAMENT

The 1974 format was retained. Italy looked strong in the first stage group games. In the second stage the European challenge was taken up by Holland who, even without Cruyff, reached the Final for the second time running. Argentina, under immense pressure, secured a second stage place and went on to beat Peru 6-0 to reach the Final.

THE FINALISTS	
Argentina	Mexico
Austria	Peru
Brazil	Poland
France	Scotland
Holland	Spain
Hungary	Sweden
Iran	Tunisia
Italy	W. Germany

Italy made a good start to the tournament, but only managed a 0-0 draw against W. Germany in this second stage match. They finished runners-up to Holland in their second stage group.

Argentinian fans fill the air with streams of ticker tape as the Final begins.

THE FINAL:

Argentina 3 Holland 1 (After extra time)

A crowd of 77,000 mainly frenzied Argentinians were in no doubt of the desired outcome to the Final. Their team started well and took the lead after 37 minutes with a goal by Kempes. The Dutch battled on and were rewarded with an equalizer from Nanninga after 81 minutes. But Holland couldn't muster the energy in extra time to find a winning goal. Spurred on by the home crowd, Kempes and Bertoni scored for Argentina to make them world champions for the first time.

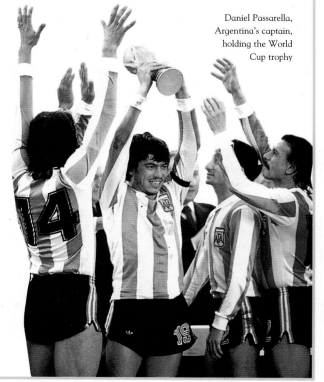

Daniel Passarella, Argentina's captain, holding the World Cup trophy

Striker Mario Kempes slots in the ball past Holland's goalkeeper, Jongbloed, to put Argentina 2-1 up in the Final.

Top goalscorers: Kempes 6 (Argentina); Rensenbrink 5 (Holland); Cubillas 5 (Peru).

79

1982 SPAIN

Lato of Poland against Scirea of Italy. Italy beat Poland 2-0 in the semifinals.

THE SPANISH ARE as fervent about football as the Argentinians and have some of the largest stadiums in the world. The 1982 finals tournament gave these great stadiums a chance to play host to some of the greatest football. The number of finalists was increased to 24. Africa and Asia were finally awarded two places each, but Europe's allocation also went up by four to thirteen. Most of the big names were there, but once again Uruguay failed to qualify.

Hungary defeating El Salvador 10-1 in the first stage. Hungary's Kiss scored a hat trick after coming on in the 57th minute.

Paolo Rossi of Italy was the top goalscorer in the finals tournament with six goals.

THE FINALISTS

Algeria	Hungary
Argentina	Italy
Austria	Kuwait
Belgium	N. Ireland
Brazil	New Zealand
Cameroon	Peru
Chile	Poland
Czech.	Scotland
El Salvador	Soviet Union
England	Spain
France	W. Germany
Honduras	Yugoslavia

THE EARLY STAGES

In the first stage the 24 teams were split into six groups of four. The top two of each group qualified for the second stage, where they were split into four groups of three. The winners of these groups then went on to knockout semifinals. There were some astonishing results in the first stage with Hungary defeating El Salvador 10-1 and Algeria beating West Germany 2-1. Brazil looked strong but were not to get through the second stage.

Algeria beating W. Germany 2-1 in the first stage. In their other two first stage group matches Algeria lost 2-0 to Austria, then beat Chile 3-2.

THE ROUTE TO THE FINAL

Italy were unimpressive in the first stage, but they qualified on goals scored. A 3-2 win against Brazil in the second stage and a 2-0 victory over Poland in the semifinals ensured them a place in the Final. In the other semifinal, West Germany defeated France on penalties.

Marco Tardelli (who scored Italy's second goal) with the cup, and captain Dino Zoff after Italy's victory

THE FINAL:

Italy 3 West Germany 1
After an uninspiring first half, with a missed penalty by Italy, Rossi scored after 56 minutes. Italy were leading by two goals 13 minutes later, and scored a third ten minutes from the end. Breitner's strike for Germany after 82 minutes was purely a consolation goal.

Paolo Rossi celebrates after scoring Italy's first goal in the Final.

⚽ Top goalscorers 1982: Rossi 6 (Italy); Rummenigge 5 (West Germany); Zico 4 (Brazil). ⚽
1986: Lineker 6 (England); Butragueño 5 (Spain); Careca 5 (Brazil).

Above, Butragueño for Spain against Denmark

Above, Denmark against Uruguay

1986 MEXICO

COLOMBIA WAS ORIGINALLY chosen to host the 1986 World Cup, but due to economic conditions this nation had to withdraw and Mexico was chosen instead. Again, there were 24 finalists, whittled down from a record 113 initial entrants. All the major footballing nations were there except Holland, and, because Mexico qualified automatically as host, the North and Central American region was represented by Canada. They had surprised everyone by winning through the qualifying stages.

THE FINALISTS	
Algeria	Mexico
Argentina	Morocco
Belgium	N. Ireland
Brazil	Paraguay
Bulgaria	Poland
Canada	Portugal
Denmark	Scotland
England	S. Korea
France	Soviet Union
Hungary	Spain
Iraq	Uruguay
Italy	W. Germany

Maradona displays his skill as he takes the ball through the England defence. Argentina won this quarter final 2-1.

THE EARLY STAGES

As in 1982, the 24 teams were split into six groups. However, this time the top two of each group and the four best third-placed teams went through to a second stage, where the tournament became a knockout competition. Denmark and Morocco were the unexpected strong outsiders of the first stage. Each won their group, but neither could make it past the second stage.

England's Gary Lineker (left) was the top goalscorer in this tournament with six goals.

THE ROUTE TO THE FINAL

Of the quarter finals, three were decided on penalties and the fourth saw Maradona score twice – once, with the controversial "hand of God" – to lead his side into the semifinals. There they defeated Belgium to face a Final with West Germany who had once again beaten France in their semifinal.

THE FINAL:
Argentina 3 West Germany 2

This was a Final that swung one way and then another. Argentina took the lead mid-way through the first half. They produced another goal just after half-time and seemed on course for a comfortable win, but 17 minutes from the end West Germany scored and nine minutes later they equalized. Extra time looked likely, but two minutes later Maradona's superb pass found Burruchaga, who scored to give Argentina their second World Cup in eight years.

1990 ITALY

Andy Townsend (left) for the Republic of Ireland and Iosif Rotariu (right) for Romania in a second stage match. Ireland won 5-4 on penalties.

Hector Marchena for Costa Rica in a second stage match against Czechoslovakia. Czechoslovakia won 4-0.

ITALY HOSTED THE WORLD CUP for a second time in 1990. With two new stadiums promised and ten to refurbish, time and money were tight, but everything was ready by the start. The number of teams entering the qualifying competition went down for the first time since 1950, but there were debut appearances in the finals tournament for the Republic of Ireland, Costa Rica, and the United Arab Emirates.

THE FINALISTS

Argentina	Rep. of Ireland
Austria	Romania
Belgium	Scotland
Brazil	S. Korea
Cameroon	Soviet Union
Colombia	Spain
Costa Rica	Sweden
Czech.	UAE
Egypt	Uruguay
England	USA
Holland	W. Germany
Italy	Yugoslavia

Cameroon players battling against Maradona of Argentina in the first match of the tournament. Surprisingly, Cameroon won 1-0.

THE EARLY STAGES

The previous format was retained and the tournament had a sensational start when Cameroon defeated holders Argentina. Cameroon topped their group and made it to the quarter finals, where they were knocked out 3-2 by England.

Argentina and Italy in their semifinal. They drew 1-1 and then Argentina won 4-3 on penalties after extra time.

THE ROUTE TO THE FINAL

Argentina qualified for the second stage as one of the best third-placed teams. In the knockout stages victories over Brazil, Yugoslavia, and Italy, the latter two on penalties, secured them a place in the Final. Their opponents were West Germany again, who had won a titanic semifinal battle against England, also on penalties.

Andreas Brehme scores the penalty for W. Germany.

Matthäus (left) and Völler (right) celebrate W. Germany's victory.

THE FINAL:

West Germany 1   Argentina 0

In a competition dominated by penalty shoot-outs, it was fitting that this Final was decided by a penalty. After 85 minutes the game was goalless and seemed to be heading for extra time when West Germany's striker Völler was brought down in the Argentinian penalty area. Brehme converted the spot kick and West Germany took the title making up for their defeat in 1986. Sadly, this World Cup Final was also the first in which players were sent off. Argentina's Monzon got the red card after 68 minutes and his team mate Dezotti was sent off three minutes from the end.

Pedro Monzon was the first of the two Argentinians to be sent off in the Final.

 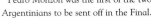

1994 USA

The amazing closing ceremony of the 1994 World Cup

FIFA MADE FOUR important changes that were intended to make the games more exciting in the 1994 World Cup. There were measures to prevent tackling from behind, the offside rule was made more lenient, injured players were to leave the pitch at once to receive medical treatment, and three points, rather than two, were to be awarded for a win in the group stage. Qualifiers for the finals tournament included Cameroon, South Korea, and newcomers Nigeria and Saudi Arabia as the representatives of Africa and Asia. Surprisingly, no countries from the United Kingdom qualified.

Roberto Baggio was one of the top goalscorers in this tournament. He scored five goals for Italy, including two in their semifinal.

THE FINALISTS

Argentina	Morocco
Belgium	Nigeria
Bolivia	Norway
Brazil	Rep. of Ireland
Bulgaria	Romania
Cameroon	Russia
Colombia	Saudi Arabia
Germany	S. Korea
Greece	Spain
Holland	Sweden
Italy	Switzerland
Mexico	USA

THE TOURNAMENT

Helped by FIFA's rule changes, this tournament was full of attacking flair. The format remained the same and in the first stage Nigeria topped their group, but were then narrowly defeated by Italy in the second stage. Italy went on to reach the Final after defeating Spain and Bulgaria. The latter side had sensationally knocked out Germany in the quarter finals. Brazil beat the USA, Holland, and then Sweden to secure their place in the Final.

Romario in a second stage match that Brazil won 1-0 against the USA. Brazil were playing football reminiscent of the great 1970 team.

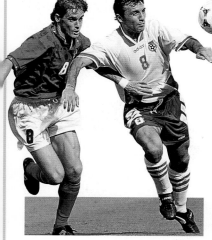

Roberto Mussi of Italy (left) and Hristo Stoichkov of Bulgaria (right) in their semifinal. Italy won 2-1.

Italy's Roberto Baggio misses the penalty and Brazil wins the 1994 World Cup.

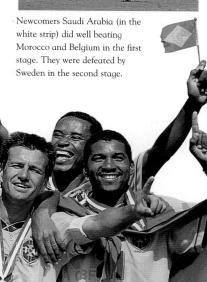

Newcomers Saudi Arabia (in the white strip) did well beating Morocco and Belgium in the first stage. They were defeated by Sweden in the second stage.

THE FINAL:

Brazil 0 Italy 0 (After extra time)

Brazil won 3-2 on penalties

Sadly, this wasn't to be a repeat of the 1970 Final. Try as they might, Brazil couldn't get past the Italians and after 120 gruelling minutes the championship was decided by a penalty shoot-out. After both sides had taken four penalties the score was 3-2 to Brazil. Italy's Roberto Baggio then had to score to save his side. Unfortunately for him, he blasted the ball over the bar, which was the cue for the partying in Brazil to begin.

 Top goalscorers: Salenko 6 (Russia); Stoichkov 6 (Bulgaria); Andersson 5 (Sweden); Baggio 5 (Italy); Romario 5 (Brazil); Klinsman 5 (Germany).

The official logo for the 1998 World Cup finals tournament

THE TEN VENUES
Paris
Parc des Princes Stadium
Saint-Denis
Stade de France
Nantes
La Beaujoire Stadium
Lens
Félix Bollaert Stadium
Bordeaux
Parc Lescure Stadium
Toulouse
Municipal Stadium
Saint-Etienne
Geoffroy-Guichard Stadium
Lyon
Gerland Stadium
Montpellier
La Mosson Stadium
Marseille
Velodrome Stadium

1998 FRANCE

With 32 teams participating, the 1998 World Cup finals will be the biggest ever. Europe will still have the highest number of places with 14. South America will have four, North and Central America will have three, while Africa has been allocated five places. Asia will have three definite finalists and the possibility of one more, as the fourth-placed Asian team will play the winners of the Oceania section for that last place. Holders Brazil and host nation France qualify automatically. The games will take place at ten venues throughout France. For the first stage of the finals, the 32 teams will be divided into eight groups of four and the four teams in each group will play each other. The top two of each group will then progress to the next stage, where the competition will continue on a knockout basis.

Created especially for the championship, the Little Cockerels are the official mascots for the 1998 World Cup.

As winners of the 1994 tournament, Brazil are among the favourites to win the 1998 World Cup.

Playing in front of home crowds, France may have an advantage.

Whose hands will lift the trophy in 1998?

More than two million fans are expected to attend the 1998 World Cup, with 37 billion people watching it on television.

Based on their previous World Cup performances and their European Championship win in 1996, Germany's chances are good.

PREDICTIONS

Many would agree that the three favourite sides to win the 1998 World Cup are France, Brazil, and Germany. Argentina and Italy are also widely considered to be strong contenders. But, with more teams than ever competing in the tournament, there may be a completely new name on the World Cup trophy come 12 July 1998. Whatever happens, fans all around the globe are in for a feast of football.

WORLD CUP TRIVIA

FROM BIZARRE EVENTS to record-breaking moments, the World Cup has produced many memorable incidents over the years. Here are some of the most notable.

1930

• Romania played Peru in front of 300 people – the smallest crowd to attend a match in a World Cup finals tournament.
• Guillermo Stabile scored the first ever hat trick in a World Cup finals in Argentina's 6-3 win against Mexico.

1934

• Both Italy and Czechoslovakia were captained by their goalkeepers in the Final.
• Uruguay did not defend their 1930 World Cup title. Upset by Europe's reluctance to participate in 1930 and with players on strike at home, they didn't enter.

1938

• Austria's team qualified, but by the time of the finals Austria was no longer a separate country and had to withdraw.
• In the second stage match between Brazil and Czechoslovakia five players were injured and three were sent off.

1950

• India refused to take part after they were told by FIFA that players would have to wear boots in the finals tournament.
• Brazil were so confident of winning the Final against Uruguay that they had a victory song written before the game.

1954

• Austria beat Switzerland 7-5 in the quarter finals. This match stands as the highest scoring in a World Cup finals tournament.
• Uruguay's 4-2 defeat by Hungary in the semifinals was their first in a World Cup finals.
• Fritz and Ottmar Walter were the first brothers to win World Cup medals when Germany beat Hungary 3-2 in the Final.

1958

• For the first time, the finals were fully covered by television.
• Just Fontaine expected to be a reserve player for France. He only got a first team place due to an injury to striker Rene Biliard and went on to score 13 goals in the finals tournament.

1962

• The match between Italy and Chile became known as the "Battle of Santiago" after two Italian players were sent off.
• Masek's goal for Czechoslovakia after 15 seconds of their match against Mexico is the fastest ever scored in a World Cup finals.

1966

• The Mexican goalkeeper Antonio Carbajal played in a fifth World Cup finals tournament – a record number of World Cup appearances.
• The host nation won the World Cup trophy for the first time in 32 years.

1970

• Red and yellow cards were used for the first time.
• In a first stage match between Mexico and El Salvador, Mexico scored after taking a free kick that the referee had in fact awarded to El Salvador. The goal was allowed.

1974

• Scotland drew all three of their games in their first stage group, but did not qualify for the next stage. However, they ended up the only team not to lose a game in the finals tournament.
• Chile's Carlos Caszely became the first player to receive a red card in a World Cup finals in a match against West Germany.

1978

• Dutch player Rene Van der Kerkhof played in the Final with a plaster cast on his arm.
• Commercials on Argentinian TV urged people to be on their best behaviour during the finals tournament.

1982

• Hungary's Laszlo Kiss scored the fastest ever hat trick in a World Cup finals tournament when he took just nine minutes to score his three goals against El Salvador in a first stage match.

1986

• The Final saw West Germany play in their green strip for the only time in their six Final appearances.
• Argentina's manager, Carlos Bilardo, was also a qualified doctor at the time of the World Cup.

1990

• Argentina's Diego Maradona won the unfortunate title of most-fouled player in this World Cup finals tournament after he was on the receiving end of no less than 53 unfair challenges.

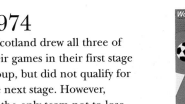

1994

• The Pontiac Silverdrome near Detroit staged the first indoor matches at a World Cup finals tournament.
• Bulgaria, who had never won a match in a finals before this one, got to the semifinals.
• FIFA's new rule changes helped to produce a record 235 bookings.

UK WINNERS SINCE 1950

Where two teams are listed followed by scores, the first named team is the winner.

LEAGUE WINNERS

English League, First Division
1950-51 Tottenham H
1951-52 Manchester Utd
1952-53 Arsenal
1953-54 Wolves
1954-55 Chelsea
1955-56 Manchester Utd
1956-57 Manchester Utd
1957-58 Wolves
1958-59 Wolves
1959-60 Burnley
1960-61 Tottenham H
1961-62 Ipswich T
1962-63 Everton
1963-64 Liverpool
1964-65 Manchester Utd
1965-66 Liverpool
1966-67 Manchester Utd
1967-68 Manchester C
1968-69 Leeds Utd
1969-70 Everton
1970-71 Arsenal
1971-72 Derby County
1972-73 Liverpool
1973-74 Leeds Utd
1974-75 Derby County
1975-76 Liverpool
1976-77 Liverpool
1977-78 Nottm Forest
1978-79 Liverpool
1979-80 Liverpool
1980-81 Aston Villa
1981-82 Liverpool
1982-83 Liverpool
1983-84 Liverpool
1984-85 Everton
1985-86 Liverpool
1986-87 Everton
1987-88 Liverpool
1988-89 Arsenal
1989-90 Liverpool
1990-91 Arsenal
1991-92 Leeds Utd

English FA Premier League
1992-93 Manchester Utd
1993-94 Manchester Utd
1994-95 Blackburn R
1995-96 Manchester Utd
1996-97 Manchester Utd

Scottish League Champions First Division
1950-51 Hibernian
1951-52 Hibernian
1952-53 Rangers
1953-54 Celtic
1954-55 Aberdeen
1955-56 Rangers
1956-57 Rangers
1957-58 Hearts
1958-59 Rangers
1959-60 Hearts
1960-61 Rangers
1961-62 Dundee
1962-63 Rangers
1963-64 Rangers
1964-65 Kilmarnock
1965-66 Celtic
1966-67 Celtic
1967-68 Celtic
1968-69 Celtic
1969-70 Celtic
1970-71 Celtic
1971-72 Celtic
1972-73 Celtic
1973-74 Celtic
1974-75 Rangers

Scottish Premier Division
1975-76 Rangers
1976-77 Celtic
1977-78 Rangers
1978-79 Celtic
1979-80 Aberdeen
1980-81 Celtic
1981-82 Celtic
1982-83 Dundee Utd
1983-84 Aberdeen
1984-85 Aberdeen
1985-86 Celtic
1986-87 Rangers
1987-88 Celtic
1988-89 Rangers

1989-90 Rangers
1990-91 Rangers
1991-92 Rangers
1992-93 Rangers
1993-94 Rangers
1994-95 Rangers
1995-96 Rangers
1996-97 Rangers

League of Wales
1993 Cwmbran Town
1994 Bangor C
1995 Bangor C
1996 Barry T
1997 Barry T

Northern Ireland League Champions
1950 Linfield
1951 Glentoran
1952 Glenavon
1953 Glentoran
1954 Linfield
1955 Linfield
1956 Linfield
1957 Glentoran
1958 Árds
1959 Linfield
1960 Glenavon
1961 Linfield
1962 Linfield
1963 Distillery
1964 Glentoran
1965 Derry City
1966 Linfield
1967 Glentoran
1968 Glentoran
1969 Linfield
1970 Glentoran
1971 Linfield
1972 Glentoran
1973 Crusaders
1974 Coleraine
1975 Crusaders
1976 Crusaders
1977 Glentoran
1978 Linfield
1979 Linfield
1980 Linfield
1981 Linfield
1982 Linfield
1983 Linfield
1984 Linfield
1985 Linfield
1986 Linfield
1987 Linfield
1988 Glentoran
1989 Linfield
1990 Portadown
1991 Portadown
1992 Glentoran
1993 Linfield
1994 Linfield
1995 Crusaders
1996 Portadown
1997 Crusaders

CUP WINNERS

English League Cup
1961 Aston Villa Rotherham Utd 0-2, 3-0
1962 Norwich C Rochdale 3-0, 1-0
1963 Birmingham C Aston Villa 3-1, 0-0
1964 Leicester C Stoke C 1-1, 3-2
1965 Chelsea Leicester C 3-2, 0-0
1966 WBA West Ham Utd 1-2, 4-1
1967 QPR WBA 3-2
1968 Leeds Utd Arsenal 1-0
1969 Swindon T Arsenal 3-1
1970 Manchester C WBA 2-1
1971 Tottenham H Aston Villa 2-1
1972 Stoke C Chelsea 2-1
1973 Tottenham H Norwich C 1-0
1974 Wolves Manchester C 2-1
1975 Aston Villa Norwich C 1-0
1976 Manchester C Newcastle Utd 2-1
1977 Aston Villa Everton 0-0, 1-1, 3-2
1978 Nottm Forest Liverpool 0-0, 1-0
1979 Nottm Forest Southampton 3-2
1980 Wolves Nottm Forest 1-0
1981 Liverpool West Ham Utd 1-1, 2-1

English FA Cup
1950 Arsenal Liverpool 2-0
1951 Newcastle Utd Blackpool 2-0
1952 Newcastle Utd Arsenal 1-0
1953 Blackpool Bolton W 4-3
1954 WBA Preston NE 3-2
1955 Newcastle Utd Manchester C 3-1
1956 Manchester C Birmingham C 3-1
1957 Aston Villa Manchester Utd 2-1
1958 Bolton W Manchester Utd 2-0
1959 Nottm Forest Luton T 2-1
1960 Wolves Blackburn R 3-0
1961 Tottenham H Leicester C 2-0
1962 Tottenham H Burnley 3-1
1963 Manchester Utd Leicester C 3-1
1964 West Ham Utd Preston NE 3-2
1965 Liverpool Leeds Utd 2-1
1966 Everton Sheffield Wednesday 3-2
1967 Tottenham H Chelsea 2-1
1968 WBA Everton 1-0
1969 Manchester C Leicester C 1-0
1970 Chelsea Leeds Utd 2-2, 2-1
1971 Arsenal Liverpool 2-1
1972 Leeds Utd Arsenal 1-0
1973 Sunderland Leeds Utd 1-0
1974 Liverpool Newcastle Utd 3-0
1975 West Ham Utd Fulham 2-0
1976 Southampton Manchester Utd 1-0
1977 Manchester Utd Liverpool 2-1
1978 Ipswich T Arsenal 1-0
1979 Arsenal Manchester Utd 3-2
1980 West Ham Utd Arsenal 1-0
1981 Tottenham H Manchester C 1-1, 3-2

1982 Tottenham H QPR 1-1, 1-0
1983 Manchester Utd Brighton & HA 2-2, 4-0
1984 Everton Watford 2-0
1985 Manchester Utd Everton 1-0
1986 Liverpool Everton 3-1
1987 Coventry C Tottenham H 3-2
1988 Wimbledon Liverpool 1-0
1989 Liverpool Everton 3-2
1990 Manchester Utd Crystal Palace 3-3, 1-0
1991 Tottenham H Nottm Forest 2-1
1992 Liverpool Sunderland 2-0
1993 Arsenal Sheffield Wednesday 1-1, 2-1
1994 Manchester Utd Chelsea 4-0
1995 Everton Manchester Utd 1-0
1996 Manchester Utd Liverpool 1-0
1997 Chelsea Middlesbrough 2-0

Scottish League Cup
1950-51 Motherwell Hibernian 3-0
1951-52 Dundee Rangers 3-2
1952-53 Dundee Kilmarnock 2-0
1953-54 East Fife Partick T 3-2
1954-55 Hearts Motherwell 4-2
1955-56 Aberdeen St Mirren 2-1
1956-57 Celtic Partick T 0-0, 3-0
1957-58 Celtic Rangers 7-1
1958-59 Hearts Partick T 5-0
1959-60 Hearts Third Lanark 2-1
1960-61 Rangers Kilmarnock 2-0
1961-62 Rangers Hearts 1-1, 3-1
1962-63 Hearts Kilmarnock 1-0
1963-64 Rangers Morton 5-0
1964-65 Rangers Celtic 2-1
1965-66 Celtic Rangers 2-1
1966-67 Celtic Rangers 1-0
1967-68 Celtic Dundee 5-3
1968-69 Celtic Hibernian 6-2
1969-70 Celtic St Johnstone 1-0
1970-71 Rangers Celtic 1-0
1971-72 Partick T Celtic 4-1
1972-73 Hibernian Celtic 2-1
1973-74 Dundee Celtic 1-0
1974-75 Celtic Hibernian 6-3
1975-76 Rangers Celtic 1-0
1976-77 Aberdeen Celtic 2-1
1977-78 Rangers Celtic 2-1
1978-79 Rangers Aberdeen 2-1
1979-80 Dundee Utd Aberdeen 0-0, 3-0
1980-81 Dundee Utd Dundee 3-0
1981-82 Rangers Dundee Utd 2-1
1982-83 Celtic Rangers 2-1
1983-84 Rangers Celtic 3-2

1984-85 Rangers Dundee Utd 1-0
1985-86 Aberdeen Hibernian 3-0
1986-87 Rangers Celtic 2-1
1987-88 Rangers Aberdeen 3-3
1988-89 Rangers Aberdeen 3-2
1989-90 Aberdeen Rangers 2-1
1990-91 Rangers Celtic 2-1
1991-92 Hibernian Dunfermline A 2-0
1992-93 Rangers Aberdeen 2-1
1993-94 Rangers Hibernian 2-1
1994-95 Raith Rovers Celtic 0-0
1995-96 Stenhousemuir Dundee 0-0
  (Stenhousemuir won 5-4 on
  penalties)
1996-97 Rangers Hearts 4-3

Scottish FA Cup
1950 Rangers East Fife 3-0
1951 Celtic Motherwell 1-0
1952 Motherwell Dundee 4-0
1953 Rangers Aberdeen 1-1, 1-0
1954 Celtic Aberdeen 2-1
1955 Clyde Celtic 1-1, 1-0
1956 Hearts Celtic 3-1
1957 Falkirk Kilmarnock 1-1, 2-1
1958 Clyde Hibernian 1-0
1959 St Mirren Aberdeen 3-1
1960 Rangers Kilmarnock 2-0
1961 Dunfermline A Celtic 0-0, 2-0
1962 Rangers St Mirren 2-0
1963 Rangers Celtic 1-1, 3-0
1964 Rangers Dundee 3-1
1965 Celtic Dunfermline A 3-2
1966 Rangers Celtic 0-0, 1-0
1967 Celtic Aberdeen 2-0
1968 Dunfermline A Hearts 3-1
1969 Celtic Rangers 1-1, 2-1
1970 Aberdeen Celtic 3-1
1971 Celtic Rangers 1-1, 2-1
1972 Celtic Hibernian 6-1
1973 Rangers Celtic 3-2
1974 Celtic Dundee Utd 3-0
1975 Celtic Airdrieonians 3-1
1976 Rangers Hearts 3-1
1977 Celtic Rangers 1-0
1978 Rangers Aberdeen 2-1
1979 Rangers Hibernian 0-0, 0-0, 3-2
1980 Celtic Rangers 1-0
1981 Rangers Dundee Utd 0-0, 4-1
1982 Aberdeen Rangers 4-1
1983 Aberdeen Rangers 1-0
1984 Aberdeen Celtic 2-1

1985 Celtic Dundee Utd 2-1
1986 Aberdeen Hearts 3-0
1987 St Mirren Dundee Utd 1-0
1988 Celtic Dundee Utd 2-1
1989 Celtic Rangers 1-0
1990 Aberdeen Celtic 0-0
1991 Motherwell Dundee Utd 4-3
1992 Rangers Airdrieonians 2-1
1993 Rangers Aberdeen 2-1
1994 Dundee Utd Rangers 1-0
1995 Celtic Airdrieonians 1-0
1996 Rangers Hearts 5-1
1997 Kilmarnock Falkirk 1-0

League of Wales Cup
1993 Afan Lido Caersws 1-1 (Afan
  Lido won 5-4 on penalties)
1994 Afan Lido Bangor 1-0
1995 Llansantffraid Ton Pentre 2-1
1996 Connah's Quay Nomads
  Ebbw Vale 1-0
1997 Barry T Bangor C 2-2 (Barry T
  won 4-2 on penalties)

Welsh Cup Finals
1950 Swansea T Wrexham 4-1
1951 Merthyr Tydfil Cardiff C 1-1, 3-2
1952 Rhyl Merthyr Tydfil 4-3
1953 Rhyl Chester 2-1
1954 Flint T Utd Chester 2-0
1955 Barry T Chester 1-1, 4-3
1956 Cardiff C Swansea T 3-2
1957 Wrexham Swansea T 2-1
1958 Wrexham Chester 1-1, 2-0
1959 Cardiff C Lovells Ath 2-0
1960 Wrexham Cardiff C 0-0 1-0
1961 Swansea T Bangor C 3-1
1962 Bangor C Wrexham 3-1
1963 Borough Utd Newport Co 2-1
1964 Cardiff C Bangor C 5-3
1965 Cardiff C Wrexham 8-2
1966 Swansea T Chester 2-1
1967 Cardiff C Wrexham 2-1
1968 Cardiff C Hereford Utd 6-1
1969 Cardiff C Swansea T 5-1
1970 Cardiff C Chester 5-0
1971 Cardiff C Wrexham 4-1
1972 Wrexham Cardiff C 3-2
1973 Cardiff C Bangor C 5-1
1974 Cardiff C Stourbridge 2-0
1975 Wrexham Cardiff C 5-2
1976 Cardiff C Hereford Utd 6-5
1977 Shrewsbury T Cardiff C 4-2
1978 Wrexham Bangor C 3-1
1979 Shrewsbury T Wrexham 2-1
1980 Newport Co Shrewsbury T 5-1
1981 Swansea C Hereford Utd 2-1
1982 Swansea C Cardiff C 2-1
1983 Swansea C Wrexham 4-1
1984 Shrewsbury T Wrexham 2-0
1985 Shrewsbury T Bangor C 5-1
1986 Kidderminster H Wrexham
  1-1, 2-1
1987 Merthyr Tydfil Newport Co
  2-2, 1-0
1988 Cardiff C Wrexham 1-0
1989 Swansea C Kidderminster H 5-0
1990 Hereford Utd Wrexham 2-0
1991 Swansea C Wrexham 2-0
1992 Cardiff C Hednesford T 1-0
1993 Cardiff C Rhyl 5-0
1994 Barry T Cardiff C 2-1

1995 Wrexham Cardiff C 2-1
1996 Llansantffraid Barry T 3-3
  (Llansantffraid won 3-2 on
  penalties)
1997 Barry T Cwmbran Town 2-1

Northern Irish Cup Finals
1950 Linfield Distillery 2-1
1951 Glentoran Ballymena Utd 3-1
1952 Ards Glentoran 1-0
1953 Linfield Coleraine 5-0
1954 Derry City Glentoran 1-0
1955 Dundela Glenavon 3-0
1956 Distillery Glentoran 1-0
1957 Glenavon Derry City 2-0
1958 Ballymena Utd Linfield 2-0
1959 Glenavon Ballymena Utd 2-0
1960 Linfield Ards 5-1
1961 Glenavon Linfield 5-1
1962 Linfield Portadown 4-0
1963 Linfield Distillery 2-1
1964 Derry City Glentoran 2-0
1965 Coleraine Glenavon 2-1
1966 Glentoran Linfield 2-0
1967 Crusaders Glentoran 3-1
1968 Crusaders Linfield 2-0
1969 Ards Distillery 4-2
1970 Linfield Ballymena Utd 2-1
1971 Distillery Derry City 3-0
1972 Coleraine Portadown 2-1
1973 Glentoran Linfield 3-2
1974 Ards Ballymena Utd 2-1
1975 Coleraine Linfield 1-1, 0-0, 1-0
1976 Carrick Rangers Linfield 2-1
1977 Coleraine Linfield 4-1
1978 Linfield Ballymena Utd 3-1
1979 Cliftonville Portadown 3-2
1980 Linfield Crusaders 2-0
1981 Ballymena Utd Glenavon 1-0
1982 Linfield Coleraine 2-1
1983 Glentoran Linfield 1-1, 2-1
1984 Ballymena Utd Carrick
  Rangers 4-1
1985 Glentoran Linfield 1-1, 1-0
1986 Glentoran Coleraine 2-1
1987 Glentoran Larne 1-0
1988 Glentoran Glenavon 1-0
1989 Ballymena Utd Larne 1-0
1990 Glentoran Portadown 3-1
1991 Portadown Glenavon 2-1
1992 Glenavon Linfield 2-1
1993 Bangor Ards 1-1, 1-1, 1-0
1994 Linfield Bangor 2-0
1995 Linfield Carrick
  Rangers 3-1
1996 Portadown Crusaders 2-1
1997 Glenavon Cliftonville 1-0

UK EUROPEAN COMPETITION WINNERS

European Cup
1967 Celtic Internazionale 2-1
1968 Manchester Utd
  Benfica 4-1
1977 Liverpool Borussia
  Mönchengladbach
  3-1
1978 Liverpool
  Club Brugge 1-0
1979 Nottm Forest
  Malmö 1-0

1980 Nottm Forest Hamburg 1-0
1981 Liverpool Real Madrid 1-0
1982 Aston Villa Bayern Munich 1-0
1984 Liverpool Roma 1-1 (Liverpool
  won 4-2 on penalties)

European Cup Winners' Cup
1963 Tottenham Hotspur
  Atletico Madrid 5-1
1965 West Ham United
  TSV Munich 2-0
1970 Manchester City
  Gornik Zabrze 2-1
1971 Chelsea Real Madrid 1-1, 2-1
1972 Rangers Dynamo Moscow 3-2
1983 Aberdeen Real Madrid 2-1
1985 Everton Rapid Vienna 3-1
1991 Manchester Utd Barcelona 2-1
1994 Arsenal Parma 1-0

Fairs Cup
1968 Leeds Ferencvaros 1-0, 0-0
1969 Newcastle Ujpest Dozsa 3-0,
  3-2
1970 Arsenal Anderlecht 3-1, 0-3
1971 Leeds Juventus 2-2, 1-1
  (Leeds won on away goals)

UEFA Cup
1972 Wolverhampton Tottenham H
  1-2, 1-1
1973 Liverpool Borussia 3-0, 0-2
1976 Liverpool Club Brugge 3-2, 1-1
1981 Ipswich AZ 67 Alkmaar 3-0,
  2-4
1984 Tottenham H Anderlecht 1-1,
  1-1 (Tottenham H won 4-3 on
  penalties)

European Super Cup
1977 Liverpool Hamburg 1-1, 6-0
1979 Nottm Forest Barcelona
  1-0, 1-1
1982 Aston Villa Barcelona 0-1, 3-0
1983 Aberdeen Hamburg 0-0, 2-0
1991 Manchester Utd Red Star
  Belgrade 1-0

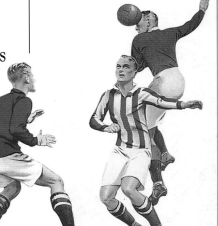

TEST YOUR KNOWLEDGE

Answers on page 96

1. Which team share their name with a mythological Greek hero?

2. When Barcelona won the Spanish League in 1985, who was their manager?

3. Why do the AC Milan team use the anglicized "Milan" rather than the Italian "Milano"?

4. Who was the manager of Scottish club Glasgow Celtic when they won the European Cup in 1967?

5. What were Manchester United originally known as?

6. How old was Stanley Matthews when he played his last game for English club Stoke City in 1965?

7. While playing in Sweden, how many goals did Michelle Akers score in 1992 to make her the top scorer in any of Sweden's professional leagues?

8. Which two brothers played for England in the 1966 World Cup Final against West Germany?

9. Whilst playing Northern Ireland in 1952, which injured Frenchman returned to the pitch without realising he'd been substituted? When did France realise that they were playing with 12 men?

10. Pele and a host of other football stars appeared in a film in 1981. What was the film's title?

11. When was Holland's biggest win and what was the score?

12. What cut short Ferenc Puskas' footballing career in Hungary and how did he come to be signed for Real Madrid in 1958?

13. Just Fontaine scored a record 13 goals for France in the 1958 World Cup finals tournament in Sweden, but in which country was he born?

14. What was the nickname of Spanish striker Emilio Butragueño?

15. Which famous Swiss club have the same name as a jumping insect?

16. Who was the first player to score in three consecutive European Championships?

17. What was the average age of Nigeria's Olympic winning team of 1996?

18. When was Spain's biggest ever victory, who was it against, and what was the score?

19. A record low of 13 people turned up to an English League match in 1921 between which two teams?

20. What is the nickname of English club side Arsenal?

21. Which team were originally called the Central Uruguayan Railway Cricket Club?

22. In which city was the first ever European Cup Final played?

23. The Soviet Union lost the first five international matches they ever played. How many goals did they score in total in these five matches?

24. Who was the first player to score a hat trick in a European Cup Final?

25. In the 1994 World Cup finals tournament in the USA, which team scored the most goals in the first stage yet failed to qualify for the latter stages?

26. Even though it was their fifth appearance in a World Cup finals tournament, which team hadn't won a single game in a World Cup until the 1994 tournament?

27. How have Portuguese club Benfica honoured their greatest ever player, Eusebio?

28. Which team won the Fair Play Award for the 1996 European Championship held in England?

29. For which national side is Heinz Hermann the most capped player?

30. Name the player whose last ever national team goal was the winner in a World Cup Final.

FOOTBALLER OF THE YEAR

European Footballer of the Year (France Football Magazine)
1956 Stanley Matthews (Blackpool)
1957 Alfredo Di Stefano (Real Madrid)
1958 Raymond Kopa (Real Madrid)
1959 Alfredo Di Stefano (Real Madrid)
1960 Luis Suarez (Barcelona)
1961 Omar Sivori (Juventus)
1962 Josef Masopust (Dukla Prague)
1963 Lev Yashin (Moscow Dynamo)
1964 Denis Law (Manchester Utd)
1965 Eusebio (Benfica)
1966 Bobby Charlton (Manchester Utd)
1967 Florian Albert (Ferencvaros)
1968 George Best (Manchester Utd)
1969 Gianni Rivera (AC Milan)
1970 Gerd Müller (Bayern Munich)
1971 Johan Cruyff (Ajax)
1972 Franz Beckenbauer (Bayern Munich)
1973 Johan Cruyff (Barcelona)
1974 Johan Cruyff (Barcelona)
1975 Oleg Blokhin (Dynamo Kiev)
1976 Franz Beckenbauer (Bayern Munich)
1977 Allan Simonsen (Borussia MG)
1978 Kevin Keegan (Hamburg)
1979 Kevin Keegan (Hamburg)
1980 Karl-Heinz Rummenigge (Bayern Munich)
1981 Karl-Heinz Rummenigge (Bayern Munich)
1982 Paolo Rossi (Juventus)
1983 Michel Platini (Juventus)
1984 Michel Platini (Juventus)
1985 Michel Platini (Juventus)
1986 Igor Belanov (Dynamo Kiev)
1987 Ruud Gullit (AC Milan)
1988 Marco Van Basten (AC Milan)
1989 Marco Van Basten (AC Milan)
1990 Lothar Matthäus (Internazionale)
1991 Jean-Pierre Papin (Marseilles)
1992 Marco Van Basten (AC Milan)
1993 Roberto Baggio (Juventus)
1994 Hristo Stoichkov (Barcelona)
1995 George Weah (AC Milan)
1996 Matthias Sammer (Borussia Dortmund)

FIFA World Footballer of the Year
1991 Lothar Matthäus (Germany)
1992 Marco Van Basten (Holland)
1993 Roberto Baggio (Italy)
1994 Romario (Brazil)
1995 George Weah (Liberia)
1996 Ronaldo (Brazil)

INTERNATIONAL WINNERS

Scores relate to Finals or play-offs. For tournaments played on a league basis, only the winning-placed teams are listed.

World Cup
1930 Uruguay 4 Argentina 2
1934 Italy 2 Czechoslovakia 1
    (after extra time)
1938 Italy 4 Hungary 2
1950 Uruguay 2 Brazil 1
1954 West Germany 3 Hungary 2
1958 Brazil 5 Sweden 2
1962 Brazil 3 Czechoslovakia 1
1966 England 4 West Germany 2
    (after extra time)
1970 Brazil 4 Italy 1
1974 West Germany 2 Holland 1
1978 Argentina 3 Holland 1
    (after extra time)
1982 Italy 3 West Germany 1
1986 Argentina 3 West Germany 2
1990 West Germany 1 Argentina 0
1994 Brazil 0 Italy 0
    (Brazil won 3-2 on penalties)

Women's World Cup
1991 USA 2 Norway 1
1995 Norway 2 Germany 0

European Championship
1960 Soviet Union 2 Yugoslavia 1
1964 Spain 2 Soviet Union 1
1968 Italy 1 Yugoslavia 1
    Replay: Italy 2 Yugoslavia 0
1972 West Germany 3 Soviet Union 0
1976 Czechoslovakia 2 West Germany 2
    (Czechoslovakia won 5-4 on penalties)
1980 West Germany 2 Belgium 1
1984 France 2 Spain 0
1988 Holland 2 Soviet Union 0
1992 Denmark 2 Germany 0
1996 Germany 1 Czech Republic 1 (Germany
    won 2-1 in sudden death shoot-out)

Copa America (originally called South American Championship)
1910 1st Argentina 2nd Uruguay
1916 1st Uruguay 2nd Argentina
1917 1st Uruguay 2nd Argentina
1919 Brazil 1 Uruguay 0
1920 1st Uruguay 2nd Argentina
1921 1st Argentina 2nd Brazil
1922 Brazil 3 Paraguay 1
1923 1st Uruguay 2nd Argentina
1924 1st Uruguay 2nd Argentina
1925 1st Argentina 2nd Brazil
1926 1st Uruguay 2nd Argentina
1927 1st Argentina 2nd Paraguay
1929 1st Argentina 2nd Paraguay
1935 1st Uruguay 2nd Argentina
1937 Argentina 2 Brazil 0
1939 1st Peru 2nd Uruguay
1941 1st Argentina 2nd Uruguay
1942 1st Uruguay 2nd Argentina
1945 1st Argentina 2nd Brazil
1946 1st Argentina 2nd Brazil
1947 1st Argentina 2nd Paraguay
1949 Brazil 7 Paraguay 0
1953 Paraguay 3 Brazil 2

1955 1st Argentina 2nd Chile
1956 1st Uruguay 2nd Chile
1957 1st Argentina 2nd Brazil
1959 1st Argentina 2nd Brazil
1963 1st Bolivia 2nd Paraguay
1967 1st Uruguay 2nd Argentina
1975 1st leg Colombia 1 Peru 0;
    2nd leg Peru 2 Colombia 0;
    play-off: Peru 1 Colombia 0
1979 1st leg Paraguay 3 Chile 0;
    2nd leg Chile 1 Paraguay 0;
    play-off: Paraguay 0 Chile 0
    (Paraguay won on goal difference)
1983 1st leg Uruguay 2 Brazil 0;
    2nd leg Brazil 1 Uruguay 1
1987 Uruguay 1 Chile 0
1989 1st Brazil 2nd Uruguay
1991 1st Argentina 2nd Brazil
1993 Argentina 2 Mexico 1
1995 Uruguay 1 Brazil 1
1997 Brazil 3 Bolivia 1

African Nations Cup
1957 Egypt 4 Ethiopia 0
1959 1st Egypt 2nd Sudan
1962 Ethiopia 4 Egypt 2
1963 Ghana 3 Sudan 0
1965 Ghana 3 Tunisia 2
1968 Congo Kinshasa (Zaire) 1 Ghana 0
1970 Sudan 1 Ghana 0
1972 Congo 3 Mali 2
1974 Zaire 2 Zambia 2
    Replay: Zaire 2 Zambia 0
1976 1st Morocco 2nd Guinea
1978 Ghana 2 Uganda 0
1980 Nigeria 3 Algeria 0
1982 Ghana 1 Libya 1
    (Ghana won 7-6 on penalties)
1984 Cameroon 3 Nigeria 0
1986 Egypt 0 Cameroon 0
    (Egypt won 5-4 on penalties)
1988 Cameroon 1 Nigeria 0
1990 Algeria 1 Nigeria 0
1992 Ivory Coast 0 Ghana 0
    (Ghana won 11-10 on penalties)
1994 Nigeria 2 Zambia 1
1996 South Africa 2 Tunisia 0

Asian Cup
1956 South Korea 2 Israel 1
1960 South Korea 3 Israel 0
1964 Israel 2 India 0
1968 Iran 3 Burma 1
1972 Iran 2 South Korea 1
1976 Iran 1 Kuwait 0
1980 Kuwait 3 South Korea 0
1984 Saudi Arabia 2 China 0
1988 Saudi Arabia 0 South Korea 0
    (Saudi Arabia won 4-3 on penalties)
1992 Japan 1 Saudi Arabia 0
1996 Saudi Arabia 0 United Arab Emirates 0
    (Saudi Arabia won 4-2 on penalties)

Central American Championship (CONCACAF)
1941 Costa Rica
1943 El Salvador
1946 Costa Rica
1948 Costa Rica
1951 Panama
1953 Costa Rica
1955 Costa Rica
1957 Haiti
1960 Costa Rica
1961 Costa Rica
1963 Costa Rica
1965 Mexico
1967 Guatemala
1969 Costa Rica
1971 Mexico
1973 Haiti
1977 Mexico
1981 Honduras
1985 Canada
1989 Costa Rica
1991 USA
1993 Mexico
1996 Mexico

Olympic Games
1908 England 2 Denmark 0
1912 England 4 Denmark 2
1920 Belgium 2 Czechoslovakia 0
1924 Uruguay 3 Switzerland 0
    Replay: Uruguay 2 Argentina 1
1928 Uruguay 1 Argentina 1
1936 Italy 2 Austria 1
1948 Sweden 3 Yugoslavia 1
1952 Hungary 2 Yugoslavia 0
1956 Soviet Union 1 Yugoslavia 0
1960 Yugoslavia 3 Denmark 1
1964 Hungary 2 Czechoslovakia 1
1968 Hungary 4 Bulgaria 1
1972 Poland 2 Hungary 1
1976 East Germany 3 Poland 1
1980 Czechoslovakia 1 East Germany 0
1984 France 2 Brazil 0
1988 Soviet Union 2 Brazil 1
1992 Spain 3 Poland 2
1996 Nigeria 3 Argentina 2
    Women's Tournament: USA 2 China 1

Asia Games
1951 India 1 Iran 0
1954 Taiwan 5 South Korea 2
1958 Taiwan 3 South Korea 2
1962 India 2 South Korea 1
1966 Burma 1 Iran 0
1970 Burma 0 South Korea 0
    (trophy shared)
1974 Iran 1 Israel 0
1978 North Korea 0 South Korea 0
    (trophy shared)
1982 Iraq 1 Kuwait 0
1986 South Korea 2 Saudi Arabia 0
1990 Iran 0 North Korea 0
    (Iran won 4-1 on penalties)
1994 Uzbekistan 4 China 2

THE MAIN LAWS OF THE GAME

Excerpts and summaries produced by DK from the 1997 Laws of the Game (approved by the International Football Association Board). Copyright © 1997 FIFA. All rights reserved by FIFA.

Law 1 The Field of Play (also see diagram below)
Flagposts
A flagpost is placed at each corner. Flagposts may also be placed at each end of the halfway line, outside the touch line.

Goals
Goals consist of two upright posts equidistant from the corner flagposts and joined at the top by a horizontal crossbar.
The goalposts and crossbars must be white.

Law 2 The Ball
The ball is spherical, made of leather or other suitable material, of a circumference between 70 cm and 68 cm, and weighs between 450 g and 410 g at the start of the match.
The ball may not be changed during the match without the authority of the referee.

Law 3 The Number of Players
A match is played by two teams, each consisting of not more than 11 players, one of whom is the goalkeeper. A match may not start if either team consists of fewer than seven players.

Between three and five substitutions may be made depending on the competition. The names of the substitutes must be given to the referee prior to the start of the match. Substitutes not so named may not take part in the match. Any of the other players may change places with the goalkeeper, provided that:
• the referee is informed before the change is made
• the change is made during a stoppage in the match.

A player who has been sent off before the kick-off may be replaced only by one of the named substitutes.

Law 4 The Players' Equipment
A player must not use equipment or wear anything which is dangerous to himself or another player (including any kind of jewellery).

The basic compulsory equipment of a player is: a jersey or shirt, shorts, stockings, shinguards, and footwear.
Shinguards are covered entirely by the stockings, are made of suitable material, and provide a reasonable degree of protection.

Each goalkeeper wears colours that distinguish him from the other players, the referee, and the assistant referees.

Any player who has been required to leave the field of play because of an infringement of this Law and who enters the field of play without the referee's permission is cautioned and shown the yellow card.

Law 5 The Referee
Each match is controlled by a referee who has full authority to enforce the Laws of the Game in connection with the match to which he has been appointed.

The referee:
• enforces the Laws of the Game
• controls the match with the assistant referees
• ensures that the ball meets the requirements of Law 2
• ensures that the players' equipment meets the requirements of Law 4
• acts as timekeeper and keeps a record of the match
• stops, suspends, or terminates the match, at his discretion, for any infringements of the Laws
• stops, suspends, or terminates the match because of outside interference of any kind
• stops the match if a player is seriously injured and ensures that he is removed from the field
• allows play to continue until the ball is out of play if a player is only slightly injured
• punishes the more serious offence when a player commits more than one offence at a time
• takes disciplinary action against players guilty of cautionable and sending-off offences
• acts on the advice of assistant referees regarding incidents that he has not seen
• restarts the match after it has been stopped.
The decisions of the referee regarding facts connected with play are final.

Law 6 The Assistant Referees
Two assistant referees are appointed whose duties, subject to the decision of the referee are to indicate:
• when the ball is out of the field of play
• which side is entitled to a corner kick, goal kick, or throw-in
• when a player may be penalized for being offside
• when a substitution is requested
• when misconduct or any other incident has occurred out of the view of the referee.

Law 7 The Duration of the Match
Periods of Play
The match lasts two equal periods of 45 minutes. Any agreement to alter the periods of play must be made before the start of play.

Half-time Interval
Players are entitled to an interval at half-time. The interval must not exceed 15 minutes. The duration of half-time may be altered only with the consent of the referee.

Allowance for time lost is made in either period for all time lost through:
• substitution
• assessment of injury
• removal of injured players
• wasting time
• any other cause.
The allowance for time lost is at the discretion of the referee.

Penalty Kick
Additional time is allowed for a penalty kick to be taken at the end of each half or at the end of periods of extra time.

Extra Time
Competition rules may provide for two further equal periods to be played.

Law 8 The Start and Restart of Play
A coin is tossed and the team that wins decides which goal it will attack in the first half.
The other team takes the kick-off to start the match. The team which wins the toss takes the kick-off to start the second half.
In the second half the teams change ends and attack the opposite goals.

Length: Maximum 120 m, minimum 90 m
Halfway line
Corner arc 1 m radius
16.5 m
16.5 m
9.15 m
11 m
7.32 m
5.5 m
5.5 m
Width: Maximum 90 m, minimum 45 m
Goal line
Goal area
Penalty mark
Penalty arc
Centre circle
Centre mark
Radius 9.15 m
Penalty area
Touch line
Corner flag

Kick Off

A kick-off is a way of starting or restarting play:
• at the start of the match
• after a goal has been scored
• at the start of the second half
• at the start of each period of extra time, where applicable.
A goal may be scored directly from the kick-off. After a team scores a goal, the kick-off is taken by the other team.

Dropped Ball

A dropped ball is a way of restarting the match after a temporary stoppage.
The referee drops the ball at the place where it was located.

Law 9 The Ball In and Out of Play

The ball is out of play when:
• it has wholly crossed the goal line or touch line whether on the ground or in the air
• play has been stopped by the referee.
The ball is in play at all other times, including when
• it rebounds from a goalpost, crossbar, or corner flagpost and remains in the field of play
• it rebounds from either the referee or assistant referee when they are on the field of play.

Law 10 The Method of Scoring

A goal is scored when the whole of the ball passes over the goal line, between the goal posts and under the crossbar.
The team scoring the greater number of goals during a match is the winner. If both teams score an equal number of goals, or if no goals are scored, the match is drawn.

For matches ending in a draw, competition rules may state provisions involving extra time or other procedures to determine the winner.

Law 11 Offside

Offside Position

It is not an offence in itself to be in an offside position.
A player is in an offside position if:
• he is nearer to his opponents' goal line than both the ball and the second last opponent.
A player is not in an offside position if:
• he is in his own half of the field of play
• he is level with the second last opponent
• he is level with the last two opponents.

Offence

A player in an offside position is only penalized if, at the moment the ball touches or is played by one of his team, he is, in the opinion of the referee, involved in active play by:
• interfering with play
• interfering with an opponent
• gaining an advantage by being in that position.

No Offence

There is no offside offence if a player receives the ball directly from:
• a goal kick
• a throw-in
• a corner kick.
For any offside offence, the referee awards an indirect free kick to the opposing team to be taken from the place where the infringement occurred.

Law 12 Fouls and Misconduct

Fouls and misconduct are penalized as follows:

Direct Free Kick

Awarded to the opposing team if a player commits any of the following offences:
• kicks or attempts to kick an opponent
• trips or attempts to trip an opponent
• jumps at an opponent
• charges an opponent
• strikes or attempts to strike an opponent
• pushes an opponent
• tackles an opponent making contact with the opponent before touching the ball
• holds an opponent
• spits at an opponent
• handles the ball deliberately (except goalkeeper).

Penalty Kick

A penalty kick is awarded if any of the above offences are committed inside a player's own penalty area.

Indirect Free Kick

An indirect free kick is awarded to the opposing team if a player, in the opinion of the referee, commits any of the following offences:
• plays in a dangerous manner
• impedes the progress of an opponent
• prevents the goalkeeper from releasing the ball from his hands.
An indirect free kick is also awarded to the opposing team if a goalkeeper, inside his own penalty area, commits any of the following offences:
• takes more than four steps while controlling the ball with his hands, before releasing it from his possession
• touches the ball again with his hands after it has been released from his possession and has not touched any other player
• touches the ball with his hands after it has been deliberately kicked to him by a team mate
• wastes time.

Disciplinary Sanctions

A player is cautioned and shown the yellow card if he commits any of the following offences:
• is guilty of unsporting behaviour
• shows dissent by word or action
• persistently infringes the Laws of the Game
• delays the restart of play
• fails to respect the required distance when play is restarted with a corner kick or free kick
• enters or re-enters the field of play without the referee's permission
• deliberately leaves the field of play without the referee's permission.

Sending-off Offences

A player is sent off and shown the red card if he commits any of the following offences:
• is guilty of serious foul play
• is guilty of violent conduct
• spits at an opponent or any other person
• denies an opponent a goal or an obvious goal-scoring opportunity by deliberately handling the ball (this does not apply to a goalkeeper within his own penalty area)
• denies an obvious goal-scoring opportunity to an opponent moving towards the player's goal by an offence punishable by a free kick or a penalty kick
• uses offensive, insulting, or abusive language
• receives a second caution in the same match.

Law 13 Free Kicks

For both direct and indirect free kicks, the ball must be stationary when the kick is taken and the kicker does not touch the ball a second time until it has touched another player.

Law 14 The Penalty Kick

A penalty kick is awarded against a team that commits one of the ten offences for which a direct free kick is awarded, inside its own penalty area and while the ball is in play.
A goal may be scored directly from a penalty kick.

Additional time is allowed for a penalty kick to be taken at the end of each half or at the end of periods of extra time.

Law 15 The Throw-In

A throw-in is a method of restarting play.
A goal cannot be scored directly from a throw-in.
A throw-in is awarded:
• when the whole of the ball passes over the touch line, either on the ground or in the air
• from the point where it crossed the touch line
• to the opponent of the player who last touched the ball.

Law 16 The Goal Kick

A goal kick is a method of restarting play.
A goal may be scored directly from a goal kick, but only against the opposing team.
A goal kick is awarded when the whole of the ball, having last touched a player of the attacking team, passes over the goal line, either on the ground or in the air, and a goal is not scored in accordance with Law 10.

Law 17 The Corner Kick

A corner kick is a method of restarting play.
A goal may be scored directly from a corner kick, but only against the opposing team.
A corner kick is awarded when the whole of the ball, having last touched a player of the defending team, passes over the goal line, either on the ground or in the air, and a goal is not scored in accordance with Law 10.

Kicks from the Penalty Mark

Taking kicks from the penalty mark is a method of determining the winning team where competition rules require there to be a winning team after the match has been drawn.

Procedure

• the referee chooses the goal at which the kicks will be taken
• the referee tosses a coin and the team whose captain wins the toss takes the first kick
• the referee keeps a record of the kicks taken
• the teams each take five kicks
• the kicks are taken alternately by the teams
• if before both teams have taken five kicks, one has scored more goals than the other could score, even if it were to complete its five kicks, no more kicks are taken
• if after both teams have taken five kicks, both have scored the same number of goals, kicks continue until one team has scored a goal more than the other from the same number of kicks
• each kick is taken by a different player and all eligible players must take a kick before any player can take a second kick
• all players, except the player taking the kick and the two goalkeepers, must remain within the centre circle.

Note: References to the male gender are for simplification and apply to both males and females.

INDEX

ACKNOWLEDGMENTS

Dorling Kindersley would like to thank:
Katherine Knight at the Football Association; adidas; Nike (UK);
Reebok; Soccer Scene, 30-31 Great Marlborough Street, Carnaby
Street, London; Umbro; UPC Sports Division.
Special thanks to Keith Cooper at FIFA.
Brihton Illustration Agency for football shirt and icon illustrations;
John Plumer for wallchart map artwork; Nicola Studdart for football
pitch illustrations on p.17, p.18, and p.90; Andy Crawford, John
Garrett, Steve Gorton, Dave King, and Gary Ombler for
photography; Richard Czapnik and Mike Buckley for jacket design;
Steve Setford for additional editorial work; and Chris Bernstein for
the index.

The author would like to thank:
David Barber at the Football Association; Steve Greenall at
Cambridge United Football Club; Richard Jones (Editor of Total
Football Magazine); Keir Radnedge; Ray Spiller; Ray Wilkins; and all
at Dorling Kindersley.

Dorling Kindersley would like to thank the following for their kind
permission to reproduce photographs:
(a=above, b=below, c=centre, l=left, r=right, t=top)

THE BOOK
Action Plus: 11cr, 12tr, c, Steve Bardens 26bl, Chris Barry 39bl,
60br, Tony Henshaw 44bl, Mike Hewitt 61br, Glyn Kirk 27cl, 28cl,
37tl, c, 47tc; **Allsport:** 26br, 29c, 30cl, bl, cr, 31bl, ca, 32cla, br, 41tl,
47br, cra, 55bl, 63c, br, 78cr, 81cra, Shaun Botterill 5tl, 19c, 35c,
55tc, 84cl, Simon Bruty 25bl, 37br, 43cb, 44bc, 82cr, 84br, David
Cannon 2tl, clb, tr, 5tl, 25tr, 35cl, 40bl, 43br, 51crb, 55cl, 66bl, 82clb,
83tr, Chris Cole 25tl, Jonathan Daniel 84cb, Stu Forster 54tr, John
Gichigi 23cb, Hulton Getty 36bl, 45tc, 46bl, 49br, 57cl, 62br, 64tr, bl,
71br, 76tr, bl, 77br, David Leah 20tl, tc, Clive Mason 54bl, Cor Mooy
39br, MSI 62tl, cr, 77cl, Craig Prentis 30tl, Gary M Prior 13br, 27ca,
cr, br, 55tl, Ben Radford 14tc, 55br, 83tl, B Stickland 83cl, Mark
Thompson 43bl, Claudio Villa 21c, 39tc; **Archiv Franta:** 71cla, t;
Archive Photos: Reuters: Michael Urban 54br; **Associated Press:**
50c; **Bongarts Sportsfotographie:** 52tr; **Colorsport:** 5bl, 9clb, 11c,
13clb, cb, 15tr, 17cl, bc, 18clb, 22cb, 23cl, 24ca, 31tr, crb, 32tr, 35tc,
37tcr, cb, 38cl, 39bc, 41cra, cr, 42cla, 44-45c, 47cr, 50cr, bl, 59bc, cr,
60tl, 62c, 63tl, 64tl, br, 66br, 68cr, bc, 74clb, bc, 76crb, 79cr, clb, bl,
br, 80tl, 80cr, 82tl, tr, bl, br, Stanley Chou 20br, 53br, bl, John
Hawkes 24bl, Olympia: 5c, 21tc, 39tl, 57tl, Olympia/Galimberti 29cl,
Tempsport/Liewig 23tl; **Comité Français d'Organisation de la Coupe
du Monde de Football 1998:** 84tl, tr; **Confederation Africaine de
Football:** 21cr; **Corbis-Bettmann/UPI:** 36cr, 76cra; **Editorial
Atlantida, Buenos Aires:** 21br, cb, 72tl, tr, cr, 79cl, 80tr; **Empics:**
Matthew Ashton 17tr, 18bl, 20cl, c, bc, 25tc, br, 31cla, 52bl, 55tr,
cra, cb, Mike Egerton 31clb, Laurence Griffiths 11crr, 14cr, Tony
Marshall 2cb, 22cl, 55cr, Don Morley 51clb, Steve Morton 28bl, br,
29br, 43c, 59br, Phil O'Brien 16tl, 40cr, Mike Poole 31bl, Presse
Sports 50cla, cra, Sven Simon 57c, Neal Simpson 2tc, 5br, 29tl,
32cra, 45bl, c, 51br, 83cb, br, Aubrey Washington 30br, 53trb,
Wilfried Witters 37cra, 58tl, 78br, 80br; **Europa Press:** 70crb; **Mary
Evans Picture Library:** 4tc, 6, 7cr, 8cbr, clb, cl, bc, 9tr, 9b, 10tl, tr, c,
46cl; **The Football Archive:** 2b, cr, br, 3, 4tl, br, 19cl, 20bl, 20-21c,
21tr, 22-23, 23tr, 24cr, 25c, 27tl, 29tr, 35crb, 40-41b, 41c, br, 43cl, tc,
45crb, 48tlb, 51c, bl, 52bc, cl, br, 53cl, bl, 56, 58cl, bl, 58-59c, 61tl,

bl, 63bl, 67tl, cra, 70tl, 72cl, br, 73cb, 75tr, cra, crb, 77tr, ca, cra, bc,
78crb, tr, c, cr, 79tl, tr, 81tl, cla, b, 85; **Gremlin Interactive Limited:**
11bc; **Bryan Horsnell:** 4tr, 9tc, 10bl, br, 71crb, 73tr, 90bl; **Hulton
Getty:** 4cra, 7tl, 8tl, 11tl, cl, brc, 17clb, bl, 18tl, cla, 28tr, 29bl, 34bl,
39cr, crb, 42bl, 45cr, 48cbr, crb, 49tl, 51tl, cb, 65tr, bl, br, 67bc, 68c,
70tr, cl, 71cra, bl, 73ca, bl, br, 74crb, 75cl, Allsport 65cl; **Kjøbenhavns
Boldklub:** 9cr; **Mark Leech:** 31cla, br, 32cl, clb, bl, 84clb; **MTI Sport
Dept:** 49tr, cr; **The Robert Opie Collection:** 8cr, 9cla, ca, cal, 10tcr,
trc, 11cl, cb, 76tl, 90tl, tr, br; **Popperfoto:** 7b, 9tl, 19cr, 22tc, 22cr, 33,
34r, 35cra, cr, 38clb, bc, 39cra, 45br, 48cl, c, cra, cr, 49bl, bc, c,
49crb, 57cr, 60cr, 61cr, 63cl, 68tl, 69, 78tl, 80bl, Bob Thomas 35br,
Tobias Rstlund 19bl; **Presse Sports:** 43cra, 51cra; **Rex Features:** 24tl;
Sporting Pictures: 11br, 12cb, bl, 16tr, 18bc, 23ca, 37tc, cr, 38br,
43cr, crb, 47tl, cb, cr, 54cl, 58bc, 60bl, 62bl, 66cl, tr, 80clb, 81c, 82cla,
83cra, crb, 84bl; **Topham Picturepoint:** 1, 14cl, 26tl, 27bl, 35bl, 48bl,
br, 50br, 67br, 70b, 73cl, 75bl, Associated Press: 74tl, cla, c, Press
Association: 5tr, cr, 76cl; **Zefa Pictures:** K Goebel 4clb, 22c.

THE WALLCHART
Allsport: Shaun Botterill: Enrique; **David Cannon:** Ronaldo;
Colorsport: Asprilla; Stanley Chou: Babayaro; **Colorsport/Tempsport:**
Christian Liewig: Saint-Denis Stadium; **Comité Français
d'Organisation de la Coupe du Monde de Football 1998:** France
1998 logo, Mascotte Officielle, Stadiums: Bordeaux, Lens, Lyon
©Berger-Ville de Lyon, Marseille, Montpellier, Nantes, Paris Parc des
Princes, Saint-Etienne Ville de Saint-Etienne Christian Bruchet;
Architects Berger/Jallou, Toulouse Ste. Absis; Architechts Ferret,
Cardette and Huet, O.H.K-Setes.Seti; IGA-BET; **Empics:** Matthew
Ashton: Sammer, Shearer; Tony Marshall: Batistuta; Neal Simpson:
Bergkamp, Stoitchkov, Zidane, Zola; **Popperfoto:** World Cup trophy.

THE JACKET
Allsport: David Cannon back cl, Simon Bruty back crb, John Gichigi
back bl; **Colorsport:** front bl; **Comité Français d'Organisation de la
Coupe du Monde de Football 1998:** back cra, belly band; **Empics:**
Matthew Ashton front tr; Sven Simon back br, Neal Simpson front
br, back tr; **The Football Archive:** back tl, bc; **Popperfoto:** front tl,
belly band; **Sporting Pictures:** spine, front cr.

Answers to national team questions
p.34 Mario Zagalo. p.35 Brazil defeated Bolivia 3-1. p.36 Hamburg
in 1983 and Borussia Dortmund in 1997. p.37 Uli Stielike in 1982.
p.38 North Korea. p.39 Bolt. p.40 Argentina 3 Uruguay 2.
p.41 Argentina defeated the USA 6-1. p.42 Bellone. p.43 Mexico.
p.44 Van Basten. p.45 Feyenoord (beat Celtic 2-1 in 1970).
p. 46 0-0. p. 47 Bryan Robson. p.48 Nasazzi. p.49 Austria p.50 Oleg
Blokhin in 1975. p.51 Barcelona: 22 times, Real Madrid: 17 times.
p.52 Denmark in 1985. p.53 Green Eagles.

Answers to Test Your Knowledge quiz, p.88
1. Ajax of Amsterdam. 2. Terry Venables. 3. The team was founded
by an Englishman. 4. Jock Stein. 5. Newton Heath. 6. 50 years old.
7. 43 goals. 8. Bobby and Jack Charlton. 9. Bonifaci. Half-time.
10. Escape To Victory. 11. 1912. 9-0 (they defeated Finland). 12. The
Hungarian Revolution. (He was in western Europe at the time and
stayed on.) 13. Morocco. 14. The Vulture. 15. Grasshoppers of
Zurich. 16. Jürgen Klinsmann. 17. 21 years of age. 18. 1933.
Bulgaria. Spain defeated Bulgaria 13-0. 19. Stockport County and
Leicester City (at Old Trafford). 20. The Gunners. 21. Penarol of
Montevideo. 22. Paris in 1956. 23. 2 goals (they conceded 43).
24. Ferenc Puskas in the 1960 Final. 25. Russia. 26. Bulgaria. 27. By
erecting a statue of him at the entrance to their stadium. 28. England.
29. Switzerland (117 caps). 30. Gerd Müller (for W. Germany, 1974).